J A P A N

GOOD STORIES REVEAL as much, or more, about a locale as any map or guidebook. Whereabouts Press is dedicated to publishing books that will enlighten a traveler to the soul of a place. By bringing a country's stories to the English-speaking reader, we hope to convey its culture through literature. Books from Whereabouts Press are essential companions for the curious traveler, and for the person who appreciates how fine writing enhances one's experiences in the world.

"Coming newly into Spanish, I lacked two essentials—a childhood in the language, which I could never acquire, and a sense of its literature, which I could."

—Alastair Reid, *Whereabouts:*
Notes on Being a Foreigner

OTHER TRAVELER'S LITERARY COMPANIONS

JAPAN

A TRAVELER'S LITERARY COMPANION

EDITED BY

JEFFREY ANGLES & J. THOMAS RIMER

WHEREABOUTS PRESS
BERKELEY, CALIFORNIA

Copyright © 2006 by Whereabouts Press

Preface © 2006 by Jeffrey Angles and J. Thomas Rimer
Foreword ©2006 Donald Richie
(complete copyright information on page 231)

ALL RIGHTS RESERVED

Published in the United States by
Whereabouts Press
Berkeley, California
www.whereaboutspress.com

Distributed to the trade by
Consortium Book Sales & Distribution

Map of Japan by BookMatters

Many thanks to the Mie Prefectural Art Museum (Tsu, Japan) for the use
of Ushijima Noriyuki's *Kaiyakiba* for the front cover of this book.

MANUFACTURED IN THE UNITED STATES OF AMERICA

Library of Congress Cataloging-in-Publication Data

Japan / edited by Jeffrey Angles & J. Thomas Rimer;
foreword by Donald Richie.
p.   cm. — (A Traveler's literary companion ; 13)
ISBN-13: 978-1-883513-16-0 (alk. paper)
ISBN-10: 1-883513-16-2 (alk. paper)
1. Short stories, Japanese—Translations into English.
2. Japanese fiction—20th century—Translations into English.
3. Japan—Fiction. I. Angles, Jeffrey, 1971–   .
II. Rimer, J. Thomas. III. Series.
PL777.55.J36   2006
895.6'3010805—dc22   2006010590

5 4 3 2 1

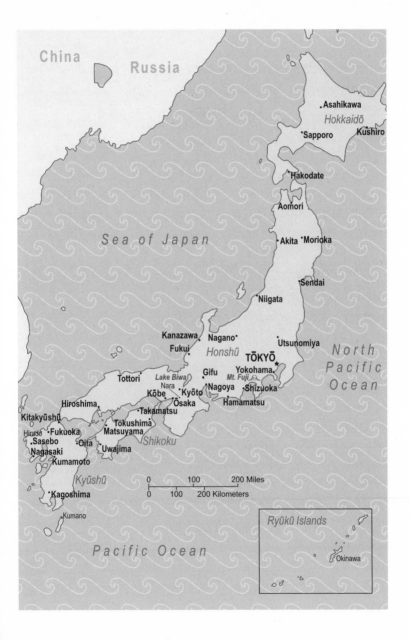

Contents

NOTE: All Japanese names in this anthology appear in the traditional order, with the surname before given name.

Foreword

Donald Richie

Japan is among the last of the so-called first-world countries to retain its sense of place. Regional differences are still celebrated despite the influences of TV, email, and the Internet that so smooth out contrasts and erase distinctions, making the proposition of one world a hideous possibility.

Much in Japan is still made of regional accents. From the cold mountain hamlets of Tōhoku to the fishing villages basking in Kyūshū, the language varies and dialects remain. The same is even true of cities. Ōsaka's remains different from Tōkyō's, and this does much to preserve a lively rivalry between the capitals of Kantō and Kansai, the east and west of Japan. A like competition between New York and Chicago is now history, but that between Japan's

---

Born in 1924, DONALD RICHIE first went to Japan just after World War II. He has made his home in Tōkyō ever since, writing on a wide variety of subjects ranging from Japanese film to literature and popular culture. The *New York Times* has called him "one of his era's most influential and ubiquitous writers on Japan" and *Time* has called him "the dean of Japan's arts critics." His *Japan Journals: 1947–2004* (Stone Bridge Press, 2004) chronicles his nearly six decades in his country of choice.

two major cities happily prospers, perhaps permitted by differences in the language itself.

With such perceived division comes a number of diverting urban legends: Tōkyō is a cold, unfriendly place; Ōsaka is distinguished only by its money grubbing. These legends owe their existence in part to interurban rivalry; more important, however, they help to define a beloved opposite.

This opposite thus negatively described is the ideal place, the fervently remembered, painfully longed-for *furusato*, a term that carries much more emotional ballast than does its translation—"hometown." This is the place from which we reluctantly came and to which we ache to return. It is a small place, and it is warm, secure, safe—all those things the outside world is so notoriously not.

That this opposite *other* should so dominate, so define the Japanese sense of place, indicates an innate balance and perhaps begins to suggest why in this madly international century Japan remains in some senses happily parochial, one of the few countries where regional deployment still makes sense.

For instance, consider defining a country's literature through its places. One could, I suppose, define American literature through an anthology that featured New York, Chicago, Las Vegas, San Francisco, and Los Angeles, but it would not mean very much because these places are all fundamentally the same.

This is, however, not (yet) true of Japan. I go to Kagoshima in the far south and ask a question of a local, ask it with my standard Tōkyō accent, only to have him shake his head in baffled negation and tell me that he does not speak English. This answer is in turn incomprehensible

to me until a friendly bystander "translates" it for me—
from Japanese to Japanese.

Though perhaps disappointed at balked communication, I am at the same time heartened by this indication that variance and diversity are still there, that the Japanese sense of place continues to exist, that difference is yet at home.

There are reasons for this. One is that the Japanese archipelago is more than half occupied by mountains and that it is really just four big islands and lots of little ones. This has meant that, until recently, communities were cut off from each other. Not only are accents different but so are ways of living and local cultures. True, that great leveler, television, is in the process of destroying these barriers that create such differences, but uniformity is still not general.

In that sense, then, this cunningly constructed anthology affirms, among other things, the nature of Japan. In the West (particularly in the United States) leaving home, making your way in the world, is still deemed somehow a virtue. In Japan (and some other Asian countries, perhaps) staying in the *furusato* and trying to return to it are somehow equal virtues.

Indeed, many of the authors represented in this anthology are attempting through their work to describe or to define their own positions in regards to the places where they were born or those that became their homes. By the act of writing, the authors embrace the *furusato*, helping to construct those internal homelands that form the cognitive map of Japan.

In Japan a sense of place retains a social value, and the differences between Tōkyō and Kyōto (as well as those between Hokkaidō and Kyūshū) are strongly perceived and consequently quite real. It is because of this that the sampler you now hold in your hands suggests a world of diversity, a small place of great variance, a paradigm of an irregular but balanced world.

Preface

As you read the stories in this volume, you may notice certain qualities that flow quietly beneath the great variety of narrative styles and thematic concerns. On the surface all of these stories, each in its own way, are contemporary in flavor, but the underlying artistic assumptions, often scarcely articulated, are grounded in the long history of Japanese literature.

Narrative fiction is no newcomer to Japan. In fact, Japan produced what is often considered the world's first psychological novel, the immensely sophisticated eleventh-century *The Tale of Genji*, written at a time when British literature had scarcely given birth to a *Beowulf*. After a millennium or more of such precedents, recent Japanese writing—which has drawn so much influence from Europe and the United States—can be perhaps best understood as a delicious icing on what is a very deep and flavorful cake.

In the case of Japan, poetry has always held pride of place. Even today the number of significant Japanese poets, both active and read, is astonishing when compared to, say, the handful of American poets widely recognized and read in this country. For a millennium the *waka* (also called the *tanka* in the modern period), a verse form of only thirty-one syllables, of which the later *haiku* is a seventeen-syllable offshoot, was the dominant verse form. In order to express as much as possible in such a short verbal span, meaning is compressed, emotional content implied, and layers of significance suggested. Little is articulated openly. This suggestive, multilayered quality of traditional Japanese poetry has shaped the prose tradition as well, so that the elusive, the lyrical, the introspective, are often more the point of a particular story than is the flow of narrative itself.

The stories included here, so typical of the best being written today, reflect little of the all too real and pressing problems of politics, international affairs, and business. (Of course, there are other areas in the Japanese intellectual establishment where such topics take center stage.) Although social pressures and problems often help shape contemporary Japanese stories, they don't usually find themselves at the center of the plot. Certainly, this is especially true when one turns to literature about physical (and spiritual) geography, which has provided the focus of this anthology.

Much premodern Japanese literature reflected a belief in the psychic and spiritual power of place, an attitude that dates back to the core of ancient Shintō, the religious sensibility that predates the coming of Buddhism to Japan in the middle of the first millennium of the common era. Many of the *waka* poems mentioned above, collected and read over the centuries in famous imperial anthologies, were concerned with natural features of the environment. In particular, many focused on famous natural settings that generation after generation of poets and writers described using a series of traditionally assigned attributes. Undoubtedly the most famous of all Japanese travel diaries, Matsuo Bashō's *Narrow Road to the Deep North*, written in the eighteenth century, reveals that the poet's travel itinerary is based almost entirely on his wish to see the famous old places named in poetry.

It is not surprising, then, that a sense of place remains surprisingly important to contemporary literature and that much of this affection for particular places comes across in the stories we have included in this volume. In this sense Japan is a perfect country for a traveler armed either with hiking boots and backpack or with a collection of short stories. Although roughly the same area as the state of California, Japan shows astonishing geographical diversity, ranging from New England–like temperatures in northern Japan and Hokkaidō to the semitropical lushness of Kyūshū. And everywhere there is the powerful presence of the mountains and the sea. It is perhaps fair to think of Japan as representing a continuum of specific places, each with its own history and beauty, and it is this specificity that gives them their imaginative power for the reader.

Japan, like every other country, has changed dramatically during the twentieth and early twenty-first centuries. Tōkyō, now the capital and the most populous metropolis in the country, was only a small village when the shōgun Tokugawa Ieyasu moved to this area in the early seventeenth century in order to establish an administrative capital far from the intrigues and precedents that plagued the Kyōto court. (The emperors continued to reside in Kyōto until the Meiji Restoration of 1868.) The village, named Edo, grew into an enormous metropolis, and in the late nineteenth century when Japan opened herself to the West, the city was renamed Tōkyō, the emperor was installed in the former shōgun's residence (now designated the imperial palace), and the newly named city now became a symbol of everything modern and progressive in what was, and to some extent still is, a deeply traditional society. In terms of physical presence, however, little remains of the old city because of the devastating earthquake of 1923 and the firebombing of Tōkyō just before the end of World War II. Visually at least, the city appears to look to the future.

Since its founding as Edo, the city has remained the center for the arts and intellectual life. In particular, it serves as the hub for writers, journalists, and publishers. Still, its somewhat overwhelming size and urban unknowability helps produce a special quality of loneliness in the midst of a family-oriented society and render life and work in the city disquieting for many. This quality is perfectly captured in Hino Keizō's story "Jacob's Tōkyō Ladder." Behind Tōkyō's broad boulevards and high-rise buildings, however, remain many touches of an older and less imposing urban space with small parks, coffee houses, and little apartments, shops, and hotels. This more intimate and modest side provides an endearing setting for Maruya Saiichi's "The Obtuse Young Man," where the possibilities of quiet walks and local festivals create an evocative background for human interaction.

If Tōkyō is democratic and modern, Kyōto, the old capital, in the center of Japan, retains more of its ancient, aristocratic past. Undestroyed by the war, the elegance of its architecture and gardens remains world famous. Its beautiful spots of ancient serenity, however, are surrounded by an ever-changing, postmodern city, serviced by high-speed bullet trains and hotels that offer the utmost in contemporary luxury. Atōda Takashi's story "The Destiny of Shoes," while dealing with the mores of contemporary society, takes the reader to some of the old sights of the city, with their considerable charm, as well as into the hotels of the modern city that has grown around them.

Another of the great Japanese cities is Ōsaka, long an important port and the seat of a thriving merchant culture for several centuries. There the merchant class received its first literary fame through the humorous and satiric writings of Ihara Saikaku in the eighteenth century. Miyamoto Teru's story "The Swallows' Nest" shows a more modern and gritty view of the city and the life that pulses through its busy streets. Yet even here the environment has an attractive energy and, occasionally, a colorful lyric thrust gives a literary flair to this modest portrait of the city's struggling citizens. "The City of Trees" by Oda Sakunosuke, an author well known for loving depictions of his native Ōsaka, also focuses on the common people who inhabit the streets and shops of this great city. First published in 1944, this story evokes the elegiac image of a place greener than the one that sprang up after the incendiary bombs of World War II leveled much of the city.

Kōbe, another seaport near Ōsaka, is now home to a new international airport and has long been a favored spot for foreigners living in Japan. Houses constructed in semi-Western style were built on the bluffs overlooking the city more than a century ago and, thankfully, most survived the devastating earthquake of 1995. Elegant suburbs that lie between Ōsaka and Kōbe and between the mountains to the north and the sea to the south offer some of the most attractive and highly livable residential areas in the country. These suburban areas have attracted such writers as the novelist Tanizaki Jun'ichirō and, more recently, the poet Tada Chimako, whose brief memoir "The Garden that Spirited My Dog Away" speaks with a special modest charm of the area's sharply sloping hills.

Stories set outside the urban areas provide another sense of Japan—one that is closer to nature and that suggests the latent power and sometimes mysterious power of the countryside. Traveling north from the huge metropolis of Tōkyō, one comes to one of the more remote areas of the country. For many centuries before rapid trains started to collapse the distances between remote corners of the country, travel there was slow and awkward, as Bashō acknowledged in his diary. Inoue Yasushi, one of the doyens of postwar writers, evokes this remote geography in his historical story "Under the Shadow of Mt. Bandai," which describes an area of great natural beauty that is now only several hours north of Tokyo by rapid train. The volcanic eruption portrayed here suggests the sometimes insignificant place of human beings next to the vast forces of nature.

If northern Honshū brings snow, the southernmost of the four main islands, Kyūshū, brings warmth and a special energy. The area has a rich history. Early contacts with the Europeans began when Christian missionaries came to Hirado and other southern ports in the sixteenth century. Later, after Japan was closed to the rest of the world in the early seventeenth century, a trickle of Dutch, Koreans, and

Chinese continued to visit the city during the long peaceful Tokugawa period. And of course Nagasaki became still more well known because of its unfortunate fate as the second city in the history of the world to experience an atom bomb firsthand.

For writers and the intelligentsia of Tōkyō, Kyūshū may seem very far away. Indeed, it is so far that, as suggested in the remarkable story "Yumiura" by Kawabata Yasunari, Japan's first winner of the Nobel Prize for Literature, the area can take on a fabled life of its own not circumscribed by mere physical geography. And although Tōkyō draws artists and intellectuals, many of these new citizens of the capital migrate from more rural places that they do not forget, as the poet Takahashi Mutsuo suggests in his evocative essay "The Snow of Memory" about his youth in rural northern Kyūshū.

Halfway between Kyūshū and Taiwan lie the Ryūkyū Islands, a collection of islands that includes the isle of Okinawa. Historically, this archipelago was home to a distinct culture that was quite different from that of the Japanese and Taiwanese on either side of them. Until the nineteenth century, Okinawa paid tribute to the feudal lords in the southern part of Kyūshū but retained control over their own internal affairs, allowing the Okinawans to preserve their own unique language and culture. Although it is now a popular vacation destination for Japanese from the larger islands, in World War II, it was the site of some of the most horrific fighting because control of the islands would put Allied bombers within striking distance of mainland Japan. Because the fighting was so ferocious, memories of the large number of casualties haunt the islands even today.

Shima Tsuyoshi's short story "Bones" about a grisly discovery at a construction site suggests the varied responses of the population when these memories are accidentally disinterred.

The geographical diversity of Japan is not controlled just by the poles of north and south. Traveling from east to west also carries one across tremendously diverse terrain. Traveling south of Nara, one comes to Kumano, located on the Kii Peninsula, a region bounded by the sea and crisscrossed by formidable, jagged mountain ranges. Since ancient times, priests and religious ascetics have wandered through the back roads of this area in search of spiritual enlightenment. Hidden in its mountains are countless old temples, shrines, and stone markers celebrating the mysterious natural forces the ancient Japanese believed to inhabit this area. These strange and ghostly presences fill the pages of Nakagami Kenji's nightmarish story "The Immortal," about a *hijiri* (an esoteric Buddhist holy man) penetrating the deepest forests of Kumano. In confronting the spirits of the region, the *hijiri* also confronts the unwholesome and violent urges that haunt his sexual desires, thus forcing him to recognize his own fundamentally human side.

If one travels west from Kumano across the ridge of mountains down the spine of the main island of Honshū, one eventually comes to the Sea of Japan. Japanese sometimes refer to the area along the sea as the "Backside of Japan" (*ura Nihon*). Although this word is now considered politically incorrect, it reveals the ways in which the Japanese cultural imagination has relegated the region to a peripheral status vis-à-vis the cultural "front" of Japan, namely the Pacific and Inland Sea coast where Tōkyō, Yokohama, Nagoya, Ōsaka, and many other important cities are located. The stunning mountain landscapes of the Fukui Prefecture along the Sea of Japan serve as the setting for "One Night with Mother," an essay by Mizukami Tsutomu, a writer who elegized the Sea of Japan coast and the lives of its inhabitants in popular novels. This story, grounded in Mizukami's own childhood memories, speaks of the quiet poignancy of one boy's sexual coming-of-age in this rural province.

It is much to the regret of the editors that two of Japan's major islands, Shikoku and Hokkaidō, are not represented in this anthology. Shikoku, the most rural of Japan's four main islands, lies just off the south of Honshū. Partly because it had neither tunnel nor bridge to connect it to the mainland until relatively recently, it has been slower to modernize, and even today its economy remains somewhat more sleepy than more accessible places. Still, it is the site of tremendous natural beauty, and travelers who are circumnavigating the island on what is probably Japan's most popular Buddhist pilgrimage—the eighty-eight sites dedicated to the Bodhisattva of Mercy that ring the circumference of the island—often pause to take in some of its magnificent scenery. Hokkaidō, the northernmost of Japan's four largest islands, was sparsely settled until the late nineteenth century, and so much of its development is relatively new. Many of its towns and cities, notably Sapporo, the capital, are laid out in modern, well-planned grids, and the scenery, much prized by visitors, is more redolent of the continent of Asia—and of New England—than the more familiar landscapes of Japan to the south. The heavy winter snowfalls made Hokkaidō an ideal spot for the 1972 Winter Olympics, and even today it is a tourist destination for skiers and other fans of winter sport. Although the landscapes of both islands have been immortalized many times in poetry and prose, many of the finest descriptions appear in pieces of literature that are either too old to fit into this collection of contemporary writing or too long to fit within the limited number of pages available here.

Nonetheless, here is a smattering of the diversity of Japan, from north to south, east to west, as represented by some of its finest contemporary writers. We hope you enjoy these evocative stories, and, as you read, seek out the poetic overtones in each.

Jeffrey Angles &
J. Thomas Rimer

Jacob's Tōkyō Ladder

Hino Keizō

EVER SINCE THE NEWSPAPER where I work moved from the Yūraku-chō district to Ōtemachi near the Imperial Palace in Tōkyō, I'd gotten well acquainted with the area. Whatever subway exit stairs I might climb, I could expect to know exactly where I would come out on the street, just as I knew in the basement level of what building I could get a meal or have a cup of coffee, and until what time.

One night almost twenty years after the move, I left the newspaper building that faces the broad main street at a lit-

HINO KEIZŌ (1929–) was born in Tōkyō but spent much of his youth in Korea, then a Japanese colony. After World War II he graduated from Tōkyō University and went to work for the *Yomiuri*, Japan's—and the world's—largest daily commercial newspaper. He gained notice as a writer of fiction when one of his short stories won the Hirabayashi Taiko Literary Prize in 1973. His work often contains rich evocations of the physical environment, so much so that the backdrop serves as compelling a role as the characters themselves. This story was first published in 1996. The impressive, plaza-like complex of the Tōkyō Metropolitan Government Offices described in the story was completed in 1991, and its twin towers rise to 797 feet in height.

tle before nine. It was the rainy season, but the rain had stopped by nightfall; it was warm, yet a dampness, almost a chill mist, rose in the street from the wet pavement under my feet.

Until early evening there had been plenty of traffic on the street and pedestrians on the sidewalk. However, almost all the people who make use of the subway and walk the sidewalks of the district, with its many head offices of banks and buildings of large companies and newspapers, are employees who work in the tall buildings that stand cheek by jowl along the street. No shops or restaurants or office buildings front the street, so there were no shoppers or sightseers. No trucks were to be seen.

After eight at night employee foot traffic and the passing back and forth of black executive limos or regular cruising taxis ended and the street fell silent. I knew this from years of experience.

It's just like it always is.

I crossed over to the sidewalk across from the newspaper.

I was to meet someone in a hotel less than five minutes away, next to the Imperial Palace moat.

Some particularly grand skyscrapers gloomily lined that side of the street. These buildings were built in the latter half of the sixties and into the seventies, during the flood tide of rapid growth, and are nothing less than massive parallelepipeds, constructed with absolutely straight lines and planes, utterly without embellishment or a light touch. The steel shells of these buildings are massive and the walls thick as fortress walls, and even the relatively small rectangular windows, fitted with tempered glass from top to bottom, are set in perfect alignment vertically and horizontally.

One building in particular, the head office of a bank, has massive walls, all a dark taupe, making it look as if the whole edifice had been carved out of a mountain of volcanic rock. This night particularly, its dampish walls were almost black. They were far darker than the night sky—purple-tinged with a blush of pink—over the heart of the city.

In each building roughly half of the windows were lighted. I wondered if people could be working this late. All the light in the windows came from cold, bluish fluorescent lamps; my senses could not immediately comprehend the scene of people working late. The display lighting for the flowerbeds and trees planted near the main entrance was bright enough, but the fluorescent-style light mercilessly exposed the artificiality of what it illuminated. And this was true of the street as well. Every single leaf was so vividly new and fresh I could see the veins in them; they looked as though they were crafted of fine vinyl.

Nonetheless, to call them artificial does not mean they were like a tacky stage set you might find in some two-by-four theater. There was an omnipresence there that cannot be easily described: the tranquility that engulfs the street after a taxi has sped away at full speed toward the Ginza, leaving only the streetlights shining on the chill, brightly lighted sidewalk, the majestic silence of skyscrapers that seem to be cleaved out of cliffs.

That night, especially, the indications of this all-encompassing presence were overwhelming, painfully so. Innumerable tiny sharp needles, unseen to the eye, seemed to prick the depths of my consciousness, and its substance, now riddled with pinpricks, began to shudder. Then I suddenly became aware of what I had not been particularly conscious of for almost twenty years: there were no telephone poles on the street, and not a single company sign.

The moment I realized this fact, the street I was walking loosed its moorings in time, becoming a street out of a picture by De Chirico, then superposing itself over what I can only call an incredibly surrealistic scene of ruins by the enigmatic seventeenth-century painter Monsù Desiderio. I, myself, was abruptly overcome by a vertigo that was part terror, part ecstasy, and part dread; I had noticed moments before a person walking silently about six feet ahead of me.

I still had some time until my appointment at the hotel, so I scanned the deserted road in both directions, looked up at each and every slab of skyscraper rock to the top of the buildings (stopping and counting the stories by the rows of windows), then peered intently at the underside of the leaves on the trees along the sidewalk illuminated by the streetlights. I was walking along as at a picnic, like an inebriate, like a figure in a dream, yet the other pedestrian also continued all the while to walk along the sidewalk at my pace, ahead of me several steps.

A part of my consciousness recovered from its vertigo. *Who the hell is that?*

He (or she) was wearing a raincoat with a hood that completely covered the head. Color of coat: black. It was a very long raincoat. So much so that it reached the ankles (such a long coat was in fashion several years back). The shoes were black, too, but the heels were not high.

Which is to say, from the rear I could not tell the person's sex or age. The figure appeared to be taller than me, but these days young women who are taller than me are a dime a dozen. And men also use the quite common dark handbag.

The dominant impression was the person's bearing. It was neither masculine nor feminine. If I had to describe it, I would say it had, precisely, a bizarre sense of that street at night, a feeling particularly akin to me as I am now. Tall buildings with their perfectly flat planes and straight lines not a second out of true, fluorescent lights shining on the wet asphalt, the all-encompassing, tempered tranquility. Yet behind or deep within it the preposterously absurd grew like wildfire, a teeming mass of blackness. And I sensed something ominous in the long-black-raincoated figure before me, the back ramrod-straight, and the stride of the too-lithe legs.

I imagined a competent female employee of a large enterprise somewhere around there in her midthirties, living alone on the top floor in her condominium with a spacious balcony, but there also flickered in my imagination a company executive, an eccentric man in his late forties with long service abroad. In both cases the sense I got of their lives was extremely weak, but this didn't mean its reality was diluted. If we take the coming together and melding of the deepest stratum of the conscious and the darkest recess of the human body as the domain of the "soul," one finds a forbidding sense of reality that touches one directly.

As I walked after this strange traveling companion, my nerves, which had been pleasantly overwhelmed by the mineral spectacle about me, began gradually to tremble, cell by cell. It's nothing, I told myself, and nonchalantly quickened my pace to overtake the person striding ahead of me. The gap between us, however, shrank not at all. Was my companion lengthening his stride? Were my legs not heeding me? The other person seemed unaware of me. He was simply walking along, occasionally almost coming to a halt. It was as though he was casually trying to entice me to go somewhere.

Where? To one of the buildings on this street? Or was it somewhere outside Ōtemachi? No, it wasn't. She—or he—was not walking in a particular direction. At least I could say the person was in no hurry. The road through Ōtemachi was short. If you hurried, you'd be outside this distinctive area in no time.

Still no cars passed by, and no one emerged from the buildings or the side streets. A drizzling rain fell silently in the cold fluorescence of the streetlights, and the high-rise buildings, which all rose stolidly—though their shapes differed slightly—collapsed in on my upward gaze from both sides, reducing the indistinct night sky to a narrow slice of space. There were no stars.

I began to think that he was headed toward no specific place, that this character was inviting me to go to the far side of a De Chirico or Monsù Desiderio painting, to the heart of this street scene's tranquility. He was not moving further ahead along the sidewalk. He was trying to take me vertically—whether up or down I don't know—from "reality." The black, overly long coat swayed, inducing yet more dizziness.

It was more like walking circles in the caldera of a dormant cone volcano than on a valley floor surrounded by rugged mountain peaks. Under my feet magma simmered beneath a thin layer of sidewalk. In the twenty years I'd been coming to work along this street I hadn't once noticed the absence of telephone poles and company signs. A unique place indeed. Surely a device for measuring the earth's magnetism or the pull of gravity would fluctuate wildly here. At least during the evening.

I passed by the main entrance of any number of high-rise buildings, each of which solidifies stalwart and simple forms. The roll-down steel shutters covering the front of the buildings had been lowered. Floodlights on the structures threw the shutters into furrowed high relief. They looked as though they would be unmoved by typhoon or earthquake.

Really? This strip of land most certainly had been mudflats until several hundred years ago.

My sidewalk companion's buoyant stride beckoned me with apparent significance as, increasingly, his (or her) shoulders swayed and the hem of the long raincoat swung back and forth. The fluorescent street lighting became ever more lucid, and from time to time the raincoat appeared almost transparent. I followed my companion, all the more enthralled.

Fortunately, it seemed as though my cowalker, turning right at the intersection, was also headed for the hotel. Ahead of us after we turned was the boulevard that skirts the Imperial Palace moat, then the moat and the grove of trees on the palace grounds. The grove was thick, dense, and dark, and the taillights of cars streaming from Kudan to Hibiya and the Ginza were a vivid red. I was beginning to make out what appeared to be the figures of people going in and out of the hotel. If my companion was also going to the hotel, I would soon be able to find out who he or she was, or at least see the face.

As I turned right at the intersection, I was at last able to catch my breath, and I turned and looked behind me. The way I had come was still without any sign of life; the ridge-line of the buildings, absent the slightest tremor, and the flat surface of the street and the ubiquitous blue fluorescent light were all surreal, as though frozen, their crystalline lure beginning to permeate my body anew.

I told myself that this was nothing special, that for the briefest moment the membrane around my consciousness had merely thinned a bit, leaving me feeling a little strange. The tautness of my nerves eased and so my pace slackened accordingly, widening the distance between me and the person walking ahead of me. A bit further apart now, I could see that, though out of fashion, the too-long black raincoat was not outlandish.

I came to the boulevard that skirts the palace moat. When you cross the T-shaped intersection there, going to the left, you come right to the hotel on the corner. The signal was green. My cowalker was already starting across the street. There was no breeze, yet the hem of the long raincoat gently billowed out. I scrutinized the figure in front of me—it was, after all, going to the same hotel I was—and when I suddenly raised my gaze somewhat, I heaved an audible sigh of relief.

Further along, where the boulevard skirts the moat and cuts through the plaza in front of the palace, running straight as an arrow, Tōkyō Tower soared shining and brilliant into the sky, superimposing itself over the figure in the black, billowing raincoat. I had been here dozens of times during the day and often enough at night, yet never realized that you can see almost the entire tower, so seemingly close. The night sky near Shinbashi was murky and turbid, yet within it the tower, emitting a graceful light of silver and flame, stood steadfast and utterly vertical. Beyond the waves of raucous sound and reflected neon from the back-streets of the Ginza and the Shinbashi district, the lighted tower took on an almost holy cast. Silently it linked heaven and earth.

The instant I began to think about all this, I saw out of the corner of my eye that the pedestrian signal was beginning to flash caution. Awakening from my reverie, I quickened my step to cross the street, then noticed that the person who had been walking ahead of me had vanished.

Perhaps he's already crossed the street.

I scanned the road from the intersection to the entrance to the hotel, but the black raincoat was nowhere to be seen.

I had been enchanted with the sight of Tōkyō Tower for only a moment. In that time it would not have been possible for her, or him, to hail a taxi, for example, and get into it. At this time of night there was no building he could have entered save the hotel. I muttered to myself that it was not possible; my senses would not immediately accept what had happened, and happened on a street where, a few dozen feet in front of me, there were no other pedestrians.

Before me as I stood there stock-still and baffled, within my field of vision, I saw a silver Tōkyō Tower rising up straight and true—yet quite illusively—the abrupt intrusion of a separate "reality."

Exactly one week later they discovered cancer in me, using an ultra-high-frequency diagnostic device at the newspaper's clinic. I had had absolutely no symptoms. The doctor took one look at the image of my kidney, which had swollen abnormally before I realized anything was wrong, and grunted.

"This is not good."

Having been told the bad news, I went out the building's main entrance in a daze, and I retain no recollection at all of what Ōtemachi looked like that day. Thereafter, however, essentially unable to do any work or sleep at night, I turned over in my mind again and again that night's curious experience: the bizarre state in which I had been so vulnerable, the strange character in the black raincoat—I never knew its sex—and its abrupt disappearance. I wondered if it had been a surreptitious warning. Perhaps the mysterious dark figure that continued to walk several paces ahead of me was an accommodating harbinger of my impending fate.

I was unexpectedly reunited with Tōkyō Tower in my room on the sixth floor of the hospital in Shinanomachi that I entered soon afterward. It was almost in the center of my field of vision when I looked out the window of my room, and as night fell the tower would begin to glow. It was a bit further away and smaller than when I had seen it from the road by the palace moat but, vertical, it still gleamed placidly, silver and flame.

I was beset by severe hallucinations, auditory and visual, as I was coming out of the anesthesia after the operation. Even when uncanny, chaotically shifting hallucinatory images dominated my conscious vision—eyes open or closed—Tōkyō Tower alone continued to look the same as always and continued to talk to me: *Only a vertical shaft running from the heavens to earth will remain unchanged, no matter how much everything else falls into mad chaos.*

I know that to some extent it kept the increasingly dissonant fragments of my consciousness from final collapse. And I kept recalling a passage I'd forgotten from an ancient work, from Genesis in the Old Testament: *And he dreamed, and behold a ladder set up on the earth, and the top of it reached to heaven: and behold the angels of God ascending and descending on it.*

Six years later, again during the rainy season, I headed for the first time to Tokyo city hall in Shinjuku to get a new passport, my old one having expired; I was going abroad in connection with my work, the first time since my surgery.

I had seen the recently built city hall countless times from afar, but gazing up as I stood directly in front of it, I saw that it was indeed tall. And on all sides nothing but hotels and major firms in buildings of at least thirty stories. And on none of the building walls were there company signs or advertising. The colors differed from building to building, but they all had the same thick walls and rows of tiny windows lined up like so many embrasures in a fortress wall. And I saw no telephone poles.

It's the same as Ōtemachi! I felt myself on the verge of being drawn into another world, one unlike the everyday world I know.

I got to the place where the passport work was done by going down an escalator on the first-floor hall to an area that was like a sunken plaza, then taking another escalator in the corner to the floor below that. Plenty of people had come for passports, but because it was a spacious area I had the feeling I had lost myself in a gigantic maze. The ceiling, the floor, the walls, were the color of the sky: ash gray.

My skin was now abnormally sensitive, not so much because I was in a crowd, but rather because I was in a great open space. It was not unpleasant. The unseen stimulation, however, drained me of my vitality.

I don't know whether or not I took the escalator up after I finished with the passport, but I found myself in the sunken plaza. The plaza was indeed sunken, but overhead it was open and spacious, the two extraordinarily tall city hall building towers rising so high they seemed about to topple over on me. The walls were inlaid with a delicate, precise mosaic pattern, making it difficult to see the windows. The face of the building was not a smooth metal surface. It reminded me of a stain-covered tower of stone that was beginning to erode away, or perhaps a gigantic old tree caught in the embrace of withered vines. I could see no one in the plaza. Clouds hung low and threatening in a monsoonish sky. The top of the city hall towers seemed almost to touch the clouds.

On both sides of the main building were structures that, ring-like, surrounded the plaza to form a horseshoe. I recalled the square in front of Saint Peter's basilica in the Vatican. The row of statues of the saints on the roofs of the looping, cloister-style architecture girdled the square. Gradually the city hall building took on a religious aspect, beginning to look at its top like the spires of a gothic cathedral. I descended into a state of perception in which I saw holy statues standing in a row atop the cloister that encircled the square.

The saints had most assuredly been martyrs, but I had not lived such a sublime, near-demented life. This would doubtless still be true the day I died.

I went into a cafeteria-style restaurant I had discovered off in a corner, still with the bizarre sense of imminent enthrallment. The place was not crowded. I sat down in a seat that faced the plaza behind a large plate-glass window. The grease the french-fried potatoes had been cooked in had been stale and the iced coffee tasted like muddy water. I vacantly gazed out on my "cathedral square." It remained, as before, almost deserted. Its ashen paving stones began to undulate gently.

I had applied for a passport that would be valid for ten years. Which is to say, this was my last passport application; of that I was sure. I would not come here again; there would be no need to commit to memory the place where I had picked it up. This fact was a bit frightening and a bit depressing. A damp wind blew down on the square, then through it, as though moving on to other things.

I remembered a good friend, now dead—he may have killed himself—and a love from long ago who died young from uterine cancer. (I neither visited her when she was sick nor went to her funeral.)

It strikes me as curious indeed that I alone am still alive. The series of events six years ago, from notification to surgery and discharge from the hospital, was like something that had happened to a stranger decades earlier. How am I to live the rest of my life? How many years do I have?

It was then that I became aware of someone walking toward me across the square from the front of the city hall building. In spite of the fact that no one had been there just moments before.

What the devil?!

The figure of a man was approaching me. In a gray suit,

and wearing a necktie. A leather briefcase. He was a little taller than me and heavier. I could see his face. He was an academic who for some years had been on the newspaper's book review committee with me. We'd been good friends, although our fields of expertise were quite unrelated. He was also a bit younger than me. He was on quite firm ground both intellectually and emotionally. He was almost the direct opposite of me.

What're you up to? In a place like this?

Without thinking, I got to my feet, left the cafeteria, and ran to the edge of the plaza. I was suddenly very happy. My companion was startled, but unlike me, was not agitated.

"I had something I wanted to check out at city hall," I said, laughing with absolute naturalness.

Our houses were in the same direction from the paper, so after the biweekly meetings of the book review committee we would find ourselves in the same car taking us home. He was an honest, open sort, raising his kids as they should be raised and taking care of his elderly parents. Why would a person like him turn up, out of the blue, at this deserted plaza?

"I also have coffee here whenever I come to city hall," he said calmly. We had returned to the cafeteria and were sitting across from each other at the same table I'd been sitting at.

"When I sit here and look up," I said, speaking rapidly and still exhilarated, "the city hall building looks like towers rising up to the heavens."

·   "I get that sense, too."

"You look just as though you descended those towers."

He smiled without answering. He did not know what I

had been thinking, what I had retrieved from memory, as I had sat there by myself. Though we were good friends on the surface, our relationship was not such that I could tell him what was in my heart.

"I was surprised, too. To see you standing, all of a sudden, in front of that glass door."

I concluded it was good. Good—as I was out and about when my senses had suddenly become disordered—that this had unexpectedly happened and the one who had appeared was not just anybody, but a person I now considered to be the most human person I knew.

I had the feeling I could hear what sounded like a voice in the distance: Live your life with strength, without flinching or confusion.

I passed my gaze along the mosaic wall of the towering city hall building and looked beyond it to the clouds, which were once again hanging low over the city.

Translated by Lawrence Rogers

The Obtuse Young Man

Maruya Saiichi

THE LIBRARY CLOSED on Mondays, and was only open on Saturdays and Sundays until half past five, so the veteran members of the staff would get together on Sundays at six o'clock in the assistant librarian's office and start drinking. This sometimes happened on Saturdays as well, and occasionally the chief librarian would join them, and even some of the girls. Most of the drink was what had been received as gifts from bookshops and other places, but usually that wasn't enough, so they'd have a collection and someone would be sent out to buy more. On very rare occasions they got something to eat from a local shop.

Naturally what they talked about most was books; about

MARUYA SAIICHI (1925–) mixes philosophical sophistication with iconoclastic humor in his writing. He began his career as a scholar, teaching and writing on James Joyce and Graham Greene. His first important novel, *Sasamakura* (Grass for My Pillow, 1966), dealt with a draft evader during World War II. Maruya's reputation as a wry commentator on contemporary Japanese culture was solidified with the publication of two novels, *Tatta hitori no hanran* (A Singular Rebellion, 1972) and *Onna-zokari* (A Mature Woman, 1993). This story was first published in the literary journal *Bungakukai* (Literary World) in 1986.

books that had pages torn out of them, books that were stolen; about what was wrong with recently published dictionaries and encyclopedias. They were critical of publishers and would weigh up the various scholars who came in to borrow material for some edition they were working on. Otherwise it was just ordinary chatter.

Part of that chatter consisted of speculation about the readers. In fact one Sunday only a couple of days ago they'd begun talking about a rather good-looking girl who'd been coming to the library every day to research something to do with Meiji literature. She stood out from the others because of her well-shaped features, her white skin, and her slightly mischievous expression. She was a university student, and she'd gotten on good terms fairly quickly with a young man from another university who'd been using the library since the beginning of the summer vacation.

Every day they sat at the same table in the reading area in front of the sociology shelves. They went out to lunch and left at the end of the day together. The man read massive tomes on sociology by German scholars, and the girl read mostly poetry. The man sometimes made use of English translations, but mainly it was all in Japanese. The girl didn't appear to be making many notes but just reading for enjoyment. The one thing they knew for certain was that she was twenty and he was twenty-four.

One librarian said the girl was a real good-looker while the man was nothing to write home about; but another, an unmarried woman in her forties, was of the quite opposite opinion, being on the young man's side, and this led to some relatively heated discussion. She admitted that he couldn't be called handsome, but from a woman's point of view he was definitely attractive, and some of the men said they could see what she meant. Another said it was the girl who was enthusiastic, while the man wasn't all that interested. When it came to the crucial question of whether the two were sleeping together or not, interestingly, opinion was divided. They certainly looked friendly enough, but perhaps it was no more than that. There didn't seem to be anything more than that, anyway. For example, it wasn't all that uncommon for young couples to walk about the library nowadays hand in hand, but those two didn't. Since nobody had any particular evidence to put forward, and they'd all had a little to drink, there were people who deliberately opposed that idea, stirring up confrontation for its own sake; so it was understandable that finally there was no clear consensus. For a start, the assistant librarian, a man accustomed to using the most extreme caution in any matter requiring judgment, maintained that as he had not yet seen the couple in question, he was unable to say a word one way or the other. Still, since all the staff believed they were up on the latest fashions and behavior among the younger readers, and since they were equally convinced these things were totally different from their own university days, they had each made an assumption that was quite unfounded. The fact was that both the girl and the young man were virgins, an idea that had not once crossed the mind of any member of the library staff.

On this Tuesday morning, the girl appeared slightly later than usual, at ten thirty, when the young man was already seated in the sociology section. From the moment she'd first spotted him at the entrance, she had smiled, and she went on smiling as she walked the considerable distance to where he was seated, then sat down at his side. She was wearing a gray T-shirt, white culottes, and a necklace of large black and white square stones. It was the first time he'd seen the necklace. As it was still relatively early, the library was fairly empty and very quiet, so they said nothing to each other. They occasionally exchanged glances, or pointed to their watches and nodded, and went on reading until noon.

Around twelve o'clock the silence of the library was suddenly broken, as if all the noises of the surrounding streets had invaded the secluded place. They went to the restaurant on the fourth floor and joined the queue for meal tickets. Immediately after they'd left the reading room, the girl had started a continual flow of speech, to which the young man made only the occasional interjection. She was always like that, jumping about from one subject to another that seemed quite unrelated, but she hadn't given him the impression that she was feather-brained. She was particularly loquacious today, and he began to think that maybe the reason he didn't think her stupid was because his affection for her had muddled his judgment. Up to now whenever he heard a girl talk like that he had always assumed she was a fool.

After lunch they had coffee, then, as always, he invited her for a walk. They walked out of the crowded restaurant with its smells of cooking and cigarette smoke and into the nearby park. The rich foliage of the trees kept out the powerful rays of the burning August sun, but it was definitely not cool.

They walked round the pond, and he explained that the reason why stayed in Tōkyō for the summer and didn't go home to Ōsaka was that his father had bought him a flat in Tōkyō where he lived on his own, and as far as he was concerned the best times in Tōkyō were over the New Year period and the early weeks of August, although it was true he still hadn't actually spent the New Year period here. In August the streets were quiet, the air was clean, and you could see Mt. Fuji from the top of any high building, and he really liked that, so he thought it best not to go home until the twentieth or so. On hearing this, the girl asked him if he was that crazy about Mt. Fuji, and he made the odd reply that they didn't have one in Ōsaka.

They went up a small hill and sat down. They chose a wooden bench to sit on because the concrete one was hot and there was white dust accumulated in the hollows of it. As they sat down side by side he suddenly asked her if she wanted to go to his place since he had some CDs she'd like, and there was that collection of paintings she'd said she wanted to see. While he was explaining this proposal she raised her hand and called out, "Excuse me," like an awkward schoolgirl determined to stop a teacher in his stride. He stopped talking, and she said:

"Is there any danger involved?"

"Well, I suppose there is, a bit," he said with an embarrassed smile.

"You're honest, anyway."

"Would it bother you?"

"Danger is dangerous."

"You can say that."

"You can."

He was glad that at least she wasn't angry, so he started grumbling about the fact that he'd taken so much trouble yesterday cleaning the place up.

"I even changed the sheets."

"There you are: a real danger sign."

"Okay then, let's do it like this. I'll promise you there's no danger, and you can trust me and . . ."

"Nobody's ever going to believe that sort of promise."

"I suppose not."

"There you are, then."

"I guess so."

"For a young girl to go to a man's room is always essentially dangerous. That's how it is."

"But there can be exceptions."

"You've already admitted this won't be one of them."

"Yes."

He gave a sigh but the girl took no notice. He then sat for a while as if he were trying to think of something else to do, although what he said next was a line he'd prepared in case his first proposal fell through.

"How about going to look at a festival, then? There's one on today in Tsukudajima."

The girl's large eyes grew even larger.

"You mean that place on the other side of the Ginza?"

"That's right."

"The place the preserved food is named after?"*

"Right."

Although she was born and bred in Tōkyō, she'd never been there, so the young man from Ōsaka explained about the festival to her.

"It's a really terrific festival. Absolutely bursting with energy and all that. It's not really a Tōkyō affair at all. It's a leftover from the time when the place was a fishing village."

*_Tsukudani_: a method of preserving food by boiling it in soy sauce. _(Trans.)_

"So they still have feast days?"

"Of course they do. There's one where everybody tries to be first to touch the lion's nose because that's supposed to be lucky, and there's this tremendous scramble all over the place and some people even get injured. I haven't seen that one, though."

"The lion's nose?"

"The head of the lion they use in the lion dance."

"Do they all have those great big scarf things on their heads?"

"Sure. They all wear the same kind of *yukata*, too.[*] Really fancy designs. There're three kinds and people wear the one they like."

"In bold, exotic patterns?"

"Yeah, really striking. If you include what the children wear, then there are four kinds."

"Portable shrines?"

"What else? It's a major Sumiyoshi shrine, dedicated to the sea god. They put up those great banners with huge letters on them, and you can see them even before you get to the big bridge. Five or six, I think."

"Really? And it's today?"

"That's right. It's in my diary. I've got a three-year diary."

The girl then asked him if he'd seen the festival (he had, two years ago), and if he kept his diary regularly (he kept it most of the time but sometimes forgot to), and if he found a three-year diary useful (sure it was useful, other-

---

[*]*Yukata*: a kind of light, single-layered style of traditional dress, worn during the summer, especially at festivals. *(Trans.)*

wise he wouldn't have known about the festival today), and if he'd written about her in it (he had, but only a little), and a number of other things with a persistent inquisitiveness, before she said: "It's funny that someone from Ōsaka should know about a festival like that."

"I went with a friend."

"Someone from Tsukada?"

"Not exactly, but he was born in Tōkyō. His father runs a drapery store in the Ginza. He was in the same class as me."

"Shall we invite him along?"

"He's dead."

"Was he sick or something?"

She saw he was hesitating for an answer so she added quickly, "It must be pretty quiet in August in Ōsaka, surely?"

He was pleased she'd changed the subject.

"It's no different from normal. Nobody goes back home."

"I've never been there. Or Kōbe either."

"You see the people who come to Ōsaka from the provinces come from nearby places like Tokushima or Hyōgō, so they can go home anytime, and there's no need to go back, especially in August. They've got cars and things. . . ."

"What about Kyōto?"

"Absolutely packed. People all over the place. There's the Daimonji fire festival on the sixteenth for a start, then . . ."

"That's right. I've seen it. Was it the sixteenth? It's awfully hot in Kyōto."

The young man was about to talk of another fire festival he'd seen, but she suddenly said, "I'd like to see it. It sounds fun."

She had leaped from Kyōto to Tsukada as easily as people do in a science fiction comic, but he was not thrown by that at all and knew exactly what she meant. They collected their belongings from the locker room, and walked to the subway station down a windless street under the full glare of the sun.

The girl in her gray T-shirt and white culottes and the man in his white shirt and dark blue trousers walked toward Tsukuda Bridge in a cool breeze blowing from the river. Their faces and hands were covered with light perspiration.

"The one downriver is Kachidoki Bridge."

"I know."

"You can smell the sea, can't you?"

"I can't." Yet after she'd said that she took an absurdly serious deep breath, and said, "Maybe I can."

"You see."

But before he began to climb the steps up to the bridge he noticed with some unease that he could see no banners on the opposite bank. He screwed up his eyes in disbelief, but there wasn't even the shadow of a single white banner to be seen, only the trees on the opposite bank with the blue sky of summer above them. The first thought that occurred to him was that there must be some reason why they couldn't put up any this year, but that sounded peculiar even to himself. The next was that he might have gotten the date wrong, but that seemed totally improbable because he had a three-year diary and the space above today, last year on the same day, was empty, and above that he'd clearly recorded the fact that he'd gone to the Tsukuda festival. Perhaps they'd canceled the festival this year, but festivals don't just get canceled, and while he was hastily thinking of such possibilities and rejecting them one after the other, another awkward fact struck him. He remembered that in the vicinity of the steps up to the bridge the year before last there'd been stalls here and there selling goldfish and paper water flowers, but this year there wasn't any sign of them, and on the long, wide bridge there were only four or five people (counting both sides), and none of them had children. Wherever he looked, and as far as he looked, there was nothing to suggest a festival was taking place.

There was almost no traffic on the bridge either, just the occasional truck or car. A pleasure launch was plowing toward them from the direction of Kachidoki Bridge, and he could watch its progress quite clearly since there was so little traffic to obscure the view. The white foam at the bow looked like decoration. Both the upper and lower decks seemed to be crammed with passengers dressed in white, and those on the upper deck all appeared to be standing up for some reason. To make sure of this he stopped, and a peculiar, raw sense of the flexibility of the bridge assailed him, running through his shoes and up his body to the region of his heart. The steel, concrete, and asphalt of the bridge was gently bending and swaying, moving very slightly backward and forward. That he should experience this sensually, almost erotically, was perhaps either an indication of his romantic feelings or just a simple accompaniment of physical lust, and he wondered if the girl standing waiting at his side and looking down into the waters of the wide river was responding to the same stimulus, so he

asked her. But she only said, as if she wasn't all that interested, "Is it moving? Oh it does seem to be a bit."

The vexed young man pressed down softly once again
with the soles of his feet, and all his anxiety at there being
no festival when he'd brought her all this way to see it
seemed to be reflected and involved in the vivid response
the bridge gave him.

As soon as they reached the other side of the Sumida
River, they walked down to their left onto the island of
Tsukuda. It seemed quite unlike the view they'd seen from
the left side of the bridge of warehouses and large blocks
of flats, for these were all private houses, low buildings
creeping along both sides of the street, and in front of each
house was a variety of potted plants of all shapes and sizes,
luxuriant with foliage that soaked in the burning rays of
the sun high overhead. In front of the house directly before
them there were two upright poles with a plastic bar
stretched between them. On the poles masses of washing
had been hung out to dry, and as the wind parted this curtain of washing you caught a glimpse of a narrow entrance
hall with shelves for shoes. The glass door leading from the
hallway into the corridor was ajar and the bamboo blind
hanging there had gotten caught in the door, tilted slantwise and looking as if it had been like that all summer. A
bell hung from the upper eaves to catch the wind and
please the inhabitants with its sound. Two middle-aged
women were standing in the street having a leisurely conversation. The leaves of the potted plants were very green,
and the flowers that bloomed among them were exces-
sively yellow, while the wind-bell was made of red glass, all

so unreal that you felt you were looking at some photograph in sepia.

The girl stopped and looked around at the houses.

"Just like traveling back in time," she murmured.

"The old Tōkyō?"

"Yes. When I was small we lived in Shimodani, and that area was just like this. Could well be the same even now, I suppose. There were housewives standing around exactly like them, too."

She wanted to stand there and drink it all in, comparing each detail of it with her childhood memories, but he deliberately pretended not to notice and set off in the direction of the shrine. He was anxious to find out if there was a festival or not. He didn't ask the two housewives because it didn't seem all that easy to approach people who existed only as details in a sepia landscape.

But once he turned left, he only felt more confused. He was relieved to find one house with festival lanterns hung outside, but he couldn't work out why the whole row of houses didn't have them. There was something wrong here. Just three doors away the most important house on the street was clearly observing some kind of feast day for it had its main room open to the street and was decorated with a large hanging scroll with "Sumiyoshi Great Shrine" written on it, and with two pairs of shiny black lion's heads, one big and one small, with offerings of bottles of sake and beer. Still, the whole atmosphere was totally different than it had been two years ago, much too different. There were no elderly men lounging about in *yukata*. There were no passersby. And what had happened to the children in *yukata* with cotton candy and balloons in their hands? There was no trace of all the festive bustle and excitement, for this was just another summer's day on the island of Tsukuda, the streets silent in their noonday sleep, with no sound of far-off flutes and drums. A tabby cat came out the front door of a house that had large red cushions hung out to air on its windowsills; it stared suspiciously at the young couple, then entered the house across the street, looking for all the world as if it were the proud owner of the two houses. That made the girl smile.

As they approached the rear entrance of the shrine, the young man finally lost all hope. There should have been stalls stretching all the way from the small red bridge on the right along both sides of the street, but there wasn't even one, just a motley collection of potted plants in front of the closed houses and a remarkable number of bicycles. Nobody selling sticks of candy, toys, or photographs of film stars. No shops selling seven-flavor red pepper, no stalls for playing quoits. The only people on the bright, empty street were themselves, plus one other, a man seated on a chair on the ground floor of a grubby concrete building peeling onions.

"Look. Straight out of kabuki," said the girl as she went on walking. It was a red painted bridge with silver ornamental knobs on the posts, crossing a gloomy looking ditch, and it certainly did look like something off a stage set, as if someone had hung a backcloth there. A few small boats were moored on both sides. A plastic bag and one wooden box drifted on the semitransparent water. Two years ago he'd caught only a glimpse of both the bridge and the ditch, hidden away behind all those stalls. A faded red banner had been tied onto a concrete telegraph pole, and the girl read it slowly from behind.

"Boats for hire, ferry boats," she muttered.

"Plates, plates, thirteen plates: buy a set, we give you three," the young man replied.

"What?"

"There was a crockery stall over there," he said, pointing away from the bridge, "selling plates."

"And that's what they were chanting?"

"That's right. Sales patter. I couldn't get it out of my head for months."

"That sort of thing happens, doesn't it?"

"Then I just suddenly remembered it now. I wonder what's happened to the festival this year?"

"That's the question."

"True."

They went past the public bath, with another red cushion hung out to dry draped over a bicycle, and the boathouse (with a number of boats hung over a pole suspended between two uprights), then entered the grounds of the shrine. There was absolutely no one to be seen, just a narrow path deep in shadow extending beyond the shrine gate and its attendant guardian dogs.

"Funny sort of festival," she said, and he could do nothing but agree. Yet at that very moment, three men dressed in white traditional costume casually appeared on a rather bleak and windswept-looking music platform that could be seen some way off to the left. They began to play festive music. There was no audience whatsoever in front of the platform, but they seemed quite unconcerned as they blew the pipe and beat the drums. The young man felt a certain amount of relief at this timely apparition, but it also only increased the mystery that the whole festival was in such an extraordinarily low key.

"So they are having a festival, after all," said the girl.

The young man in his role as guide suggested they really ought to go over to the platform, since he felt sorry for the musicians who had no one to play to; but she insisted they ought to pay their respects to the god of the shrine first, then go.

The small, neat structure of the main building was as he remembered, but there was nobody here either, except for one old man in a crepe shirt and jeans who'd presumably been taking an afternoon stroll and was now quietly seated in the shade at the side of the building enjoying the cool. The young man and the girl cast a coin each into the offertory box, and clapped their hands briskly. There was no bell rope to pull. Then they walked over to the old man, said good afternoon, and asked him what was going on, and he explained that what had taken place two years ago was the great festival, which only happened every three years, and this year was what was known as a shadow festival and nobody did anything.

"Oh," said the girl with a gasp of disappointment, and her voice seemed to put an end at once to the wild festival they should have attended, to those ceremonies that signified a total renewal of heaven and earth, to that energetic upheaval of the whole social body, only to be replaced by the apprehension that the social order remained as it had been. There were to be no festivities disturbing the ordinary processes of time, which simply flowed along as smooth and peaceful as ever. The young man had to inure himself to his loss, and although he tried to persuade himself that this kind of quiet, dull version represented the true face of the village festival, this did not conceal the obvious fact he had been a total failure as a guide.

"No portable shrines. Don't make any special clothes," the old man went on.

"Not even on the actual fete day?"

"Not even then."

"So they just have the lion's head on display?"

The old man smiled and said nothing.

"I saw the terrific fight that went on two years ago."

"The shrines don't cross the river anymore, you see. Last time they did must have been back in the fifties."

The old man was thinking of festivals much older than two years ago. To put up the banners for the shrine in those days they had pillars about two hundred and fifty feet high, six of them, which they used to keep buried in that ditch there. It took all the men of the neighborhood to dig them up.

"Excuse me," the girl said very tentatively, and the young man was amused to see there was nothing of the awkward schoolgirl determined to get her teacher's attention on this occasion. "But was it all right to leave the pillars buried in the ditch?"

"It was the custom," the old man replied.

"I told her there was a festival, you see," he explained to the old man while apologizing with his eyes to the girl, "pretending I knew all about it."

But the girl merely made a jerk of her chin, implying that she wasn't going to accept any apology.

"There's nothing today," said the old man. "But tomorrow, over there," pointing to an area in front of the shrine building, "they'll be putting up banners. Not the big ones, though."

"Do they do anything?"

"The officials and the young men get together and pray at the shrine, and that's it."

"So today there's no point . . . ?"

"It's the shadow festival, you see."

The girl asked the old man a number of things. What did he mean by the shrines crossing the river? (Before they built the tide walls the young men carrying the shrines used to dive into the Sumida River with them.) Why do they only hold it once every three years? (You couldn't hold a festival of that size every year. In the old days they only held it when the haul was particularly good that year.) How did they tie the sash of the *yukata*? (Knotted dead center in front.) At this point the drums and flute stopped. The young man looked round and saw the three musicians stand up in an oddly disorganized way and drift off to the back of the platform where they disappeared. He could tell that one of them, by the way he moved, must be of a considerable age; he assumed the girl frowned because she wished now they had gone to hear the music before it finished. The young man smiled wryly, while the old man, noticing neither the frown nor the wry smile, began talking about how in the past when they brought the shrines across the water there had always been a picture in the paper, and they'd all been very proud of it.

They thanked the old man and said good-bye, and, as they loitered in the area where the banners had been set up, the young man looked in the direction of the main shrine and noticed above its bronze, gabled roof faint lines of mackerel clouds floating in the sky. As he looked up at them he remembered how his dead friend, two years ago when they were going home after the festival, had murmured that it was autumn already. Yes, it was already autumn.

They wandered around the small confines of the shrine grounds. On the music platform, with its pillars and walls of plain wood, the front curtain, red and blue stripes on a white background, drifted idly in the wind. The girl said it didn't look as if there was going to be any more music, and the young man shrugged. There was a framed card with the words "Sacred Music Place," a piece of calligraphy by Tokugawa someone or other. Since it didn't look very ancient at all they decided it must be a piece of twentieth-century work, perhaps by a grandchild of the last shōgun, Tokugawa Yoshinobu, or even a great-grandchild. There was also a stone with a poetic inscription on it, but neither of them could make it out. Next to this was a wisteria vine, although naturally the blossoms were all gone. One butterfly, looking more fragile than a scrap of tissue paper, was fluttering forlornly in the exact square of black shade. Next to it was a small shrine claiming to be efficacious for curing both smallpox and plague.

"I wonder if it really works?"

"Bound to, isn't it?"

To the left of that was another shrine dedicated to the various guardian deities of ships, and this had a small shrine gate, even a bell, but neither of them pulled the grubby, spotty rope. At both shrines the young man put two coins in the offertory box, while the girl just clapped her hands twice.

There was another small shrine to the left of the main building dedicated to the dragon god, and here was a votive tablet consisting of two snakes, one black and one red, twining together among some pink and yellow twirling clouds. The picture was further complicated by the fact that both snakes had pendant paper strips of religious significance twisted about them, as well as long, thin, protruding tongues like flames.

"Rather obscene, isn't it?" she said.

"Pure pop art," he agreed and dropped a coin in the box. She also threw in a coin, which rolled about noisily inside. After they'd both pulled the bell rope and clapped their hands, they discussed why a shrine dedicated to ships' guardian deities (and one to the dragon god) should have a bell while the one for smallpox and plague did not, but, unsurprisingly, they were unable to arrive at any satisfactory answer.

"I rang it enough times, anyway," he said, as if he felt that somehow this statement summed up the whole problem.

"Four times, to be exact," she said.

"What did you pray for?" he asked.

"Nothing," she replied.

"Same here," he said.

From the back of that small shrine a ditch ran past the left side of the main building. It was about a dozen feet across, filled with green water that reflected the sky and clouds in those places exposed to sunlight. Where the ditch came to an end it was choked with discarded earth and stones and rotting timber, and beyond it was what looked like the back of a house with washing hung out to dry. You could smell the sea here. This time the girl immediately agreed that you could. The occasional heavy splashing the water made probably had something to do with the tide.

To the right of the main building was another small shrine dedicated to the fox deity and god of harvests, with a tiny storehouse painted a coarse and brilliant white, like a woman with a too-thick layer of foundation. Behind the steel and glass of the closed doors, you could make out the shape of a glittering gold portable shrine awkwardly crammed into the dark narrow space inside; offerings of rice cakes, rice wine, peaches, and vegetables were set out before it. The stems of the spring onions had wilted heavily in the succession of fine August days. The shrine itself had two foxes stationed in front. They were poised menacingly and stared with fierce eyes, and the backs of their ears were painted red. The one on the right held a ball in its mouth, the other a scroll, both gripping them tightly with their jaws as if determined never to let them go. The girl said how a friend of hers had once been driving in Hokkaidō at night and she'd come across a silver fox, but she didn't have anything to give it to eat. She was really crazy about foxes. She even had two books of photographs of them and had been awfully upset about having such terrible bad luck.

There was nothing else to see. They walked back through the shrine grounds, under the arch of the shrine gate and along the path and out into the street. There were a few scattered houses with red festival lanterns outside. Most of the houses had old-fashioned lattice doors kept spotlessly clean and left open. The girl stopped in front of a shop selling the famous Tsukuda preserves, pondered something, and then set off walking again. When they came to the end of the street, they turned left and after a short while saw three little girls dressed in brightly colored swimming costumes. They had a large plastic bowl filled with water and were splashing about. One had a water pistol, but she wasn't very clever at handling it. The water sprayed and flashed in the sun. Next to them were two old ladies gossiping on a narrow bench. The one with the light-colored sunglasses was doing all the listening, and she nodded five times while they were walking by. There was a house with its doors and windows wide open on display for the festival, then another. There was a green well pump with a dried-out scrub brush beside it.

They went to a soba shop and asked for strawberry ices. They were the only two customers, and the shop was quiet. Not even the television was on.

The young man apologized for the mess he'd made of the day. "I'm sorry, really sorry. The whole thing was awful. I ought to write things down in more detail in my diary."

"Funny sort of excuse, if you're trying to tell me you didn't know before we even started," the girl replied, glaring at him but obviously not serious. "Still, I liked it. It was fun."

She was trying to be nice about it, and she went on to give a lengthy account of what she'd found interesting, rather as if the remarks she'd made while they'd been walking had been mere footnotes to the main text of the day, while what she was giving now was a set of lengthy appendices at the end of the book. There had been some branches of sweet oleander flowering above the ditch, and whenever she saw this flower she always felt that now it was really summer. (He hadn't even noticed it.) The eyes of the lion's head displayed in the last house they'd seen were just like those of a dog in her neighborhood. What was the difference between Tsukuda preserves and other kinds, and didn't he think that the old man in the crepe shirt and jeans mightn't possibly be the priest of the shrine? He said he didn't think it was at all likely but gradually became less and less sure about this.

The strawberry ice arrived. They broke the layer of white snow, mixed it into the red, then spooned it up into their mouths. While they ate the young man said little. He had suddenly been overpowered by a sense of his own use- lessness, that he wasn't able to work out if that old man in the crepe shirt and jeans was a priest or not, that he hadn't known if there'd be a festival at Tsukada today or not, that he hadn't noticed if there'd been sweet oleander or what- ever flowering above that ditch or not, that he'd burst out with that silly refrain about plates at a completely inap- propriate moment, and finally that he'd made no progress at all today with a girl who he was perfectly well aware liked him quite a lot. The bitter sense of failure made him much too depressed to feel like taking part in any cheerful confabulation. But that didn't prevent the girl from going on talking; and go on she did, about festivals at the fox shrine when she was a child, about her uncle who disliked snakes so much he was even unable to eat broiled eel.

By the time he'd finished his ice she still had half of hers left, but she pushed it to one side and said, in a tone of voice very different from the way she'd been speaking so far (although he didn't notice), "Well, shall we go then?"

"Better be getting home, I suppose."

"I'm not talking about home. I mean your place."

He gaped at her in surprise, and an embarrassed smile

covered her pale, brilliant face. He was so excited he
became quite flustered, asking in an irrelevantly loud voice
how much there was to pay and then, in a much quieter
voice, said thank you to the girl.

When they got outside into the sunlit street they automatically joined hands. This wasn't the first time they'd
done so, but today the touch of the girl's hand—small,
soft, and damp—seemed to provide in all its aspects a precise statement of what they were about to do.

They went up the steps to the bridge, into the breeze
from the river. They walked over the long bridge toward
the crowds of high buildings like towers. Halfway across
they suddenly slowed down.

"What's the matter?" she asked.

"I have to buy something.

"No you don't," she said with a deliberately expressionless face. "Today's safe."

He nodded with the same lack of expression on his.
They went toward the subway station.

He showed her the bathroom, making a joke about the new
bath towel he'd put out, but she didn't laugh. She only
muttered something in reply, as she seemed to be squeez-
ing herself against the wall, her body stiff and nervous. All
the life and cheerfulness she'd had until only a moment ago
had vanished, as if she had changed into a quite different
woman. He told himself he'd be better off not saying anything out of place, so he went into the bedroom, closed the
curtain, turned down the bedside lamp and switched on the
air conditioner.

She came into the living room wearing the pajamas he'd

left ready in the bathroom. They were brand new too, like the towel. Being men's pajamas, they were much too big for her, of course, making her look like a small child.

"They're all baggy," she said.

"They make you look sweet."

He wanted to say something wittily relevant but could think of nothing, so he just pushed open the bedroom door. She disappeared into the room.

He took a shower, put on the pajamas he'd been using for two nights now, and went into the bedroom. She was sitting on the bed. When he took off his pajama jacket she said, as if she were disclosing some great secret, "I've never done this before."

"Nor have I," he said.

He pushed her down onto the bed and set his mouth upon hers. Both their mouths must have tasted of strawberry ice, but neither noticed that cheap sweetness on the other's tongue, preoccupied only by the sense of touch itself, of mouth and saliva. He got up to take off his trousers and the woman lay there quite motionless, so he had considerable trouble getting her pajama jacket off, as if he were handling a corpse. He then managed to remove the trousers, but the brief, elegant panties remained, apparently sticking to her body, either because of the dampness left by the shower or because of sweat. She took those off herself.

Yet events did not progress well on the brand-new sheets. The mouth play was pleasant enough, but she didn't appear to enjoy having her breasts fondled or kissed, and when he applied his tongue to the soft part of her neck and under her arm she claimed it tickled and told him to stop. Since she groaned as she did so he thought perhaps she didn't mean it, but when he tried again he found out she did, and as he was now baffled about what he should do, he stopped using his tongue and mainly went on fondling her body with his hands, touching her unresponsive, doll-like body with fingers that scrupulously avoided any over-sensitive areas.

Then he lay on top of her and for a while enjoyed the warmth of the gentle, wildflower-like body against his limbs. The girl responded to this by pressing her cheek against his, but when he tried to enter her she protested in a peculiarly husky voice that it tickled and she couldn't bear it. The young man again interpreted this as some technique on her part to rouse his ardor, the kind of coquetry that even a virgin can be assumed to possess, but he eventually realized he had got it wrong once more. He raised his body in surprise, and the girl made as if to escape, like a bird that has been fluttering in the hand and now has the chance to be free. When he tried to hold her back, she thrust out her arm in an unconscious bid for help, managing to knock over the light on the small bedside table. The thin darkness of the room became darker. He leaned over and put the lamp back in place, whispering to her that perhaps they ought to have a break. They lay side by side, light perspiration standing out on their bodies.

The girl said she was sorry, and he apologized. Then they spoke words of encouragement, like two mountain climbers urging each other on; it would be all right so long as they didn't try to rush things and took their time. Yet when he observed the sweat soaking the girl's stomach this suddenly aroused him. He put a pillow under her thighs, while she made no resistance. She opened her white legs and raised them until her thighs pressed against her breasts; but this still didn't help because she again found the sensation unbearable, and as she jerked away her tiny foot kicked the young man on the jaw. He grunted in pain, but she was much too preoccupied to apologize. He removed the pillow from under her buttocks and folded it in front of the headboard, placing it upright at first then changing it to a slightly slantwise position. He took hold of her hips and altered her posture a little, turned up the light slightly and then, because they were still getting nowhere, made it even brighter. She didn't protest but screwed her face up in an ugly way, so this time he tried moistening the area with his tongue, but she just squirmed away, making little cries like the sound of the wind or the high treble of a flute, wriggling and sliding across the bed until her head and then her shoulders projected over the side away from the lamp. Displaying her white throat, she looked as if she were about to fall off. He pulled her helpless body back up again, and then she raised herself, her face a mass of tangled hair turned toward him, neither looking at him nor looking away; and she shook her head in apparent refusal, leaning against the headboard and the pillow placed before it. He kneeled before her, wiping the sweat from his brow with the palm of his hand.

Then it happened. A sensation often experienced since boyhood, a heavy, wavelike feeling suddenly flowed through his loins, and a thick, white thread of sperm burst from him in an arched trajectory, making violent, hot contact just below the girl's right eye. It was just as if this clammy, warm projectile had been aimed precisely at the very edge of the soft fold of her lower eyelid, or even perhaps at the eye itself, long and oval, with thick eyelashes brimming with tears, and unluckily had missed its mark. The girl automatically closed her eyes, but immediately opened them again, and, enwrapped in an odor reminiscent of armpits, sap, and pollen, she nervously felt with the fingers of her right hand this splatter of hot milk, this highly viscous gruel.

"What's this?" she muttered hoarsely, but knew immediately what it was and what had happened.

He didn't answer. The warmth of what was now more like a dribble of rather waterish gruel soon vanished, if not its powerful smell, and the thin, white liquid flowed slowly down her cheek, dividing into three streams, one of them finally arriving at her upper lip from which all the lipstick had rubbed off. The two streams that passed round the mouth dripped slowly off her chin, slid over her breasts, then made a rapid, shallow progression from her stomach to her thighs. As she stared with those fixed, smoldering eyes, the young man endured feelings of quite unforgivable shame, but he assumed an indifferent expression and said, "You know, it looks just like the patterns of those clouds and snakes." Still enveloped in that rich odor, the girl laughed noiselessly.

The next day the young man went at his usual time to the library and sat reading at his normal place. That night after what had happened, they'd gone out and had spaghetti to eat, then parted at the station but hadn't said anything about today, so he didn't know if she'd be coming or not, although he was assuming she would. In fact she hadn't come by twelve o'clock, so he took his lunch and walked alone, then went back to the reading room when, after a short while, she drifted in wearing a dress with a large flowered pattern of purple, emerald, and orange, plus a very red bracelet. He had seen the bracelet before.

There was nobody else seated at the same table, as if this had been deliberately arranged. Their chairs also were a trifle closer together than they had been up until yesterday. The girl had done this when she sat down. They both went on reading.

After quite a long while, the girl wrote something on a piece of paper and passed it to him. She had written that it was much nicer being just like this, wasn't it? When he read this he turned red with shame. Surely she didn't have to make her contempt for him so very plain, he thought, looking at her in anger. She glanced at him out of the corner of her eye, then straight at him. Quite probably she had merely meant to communicate her pleasure at sitting here like this and reading, but what the note really expressed, even if she was not herself fully aware of it, was an open sexual invitation, and yet the obtuse young man still failed to notice.

Translated by Dennis Keene

Under the Shadow of Mt. Bandai

Inoue Yasushi

IN THOSE DAYS the road from Kitakata to Hibara was a journey of some fifteen miles. By leaving Kitakata around eight o'clock in the morning and proceeding at a leisurely pace, one could be in Hibara by two or three in the afternoon. On the way, however, one crossed the Ōshio Pass just beyond Ōshio village. For some distance on both sides of the summit there was a difficult stretch that wound its way through sharp outcroppings of rock. Yet teamsters with pack animals passed this way in both directions virtually every day, and for these sturdy working men the trip was no hardship. The road, called the Yonezawa Highway, went from Wakamatsu through Kitakata and Hibara and

---

INOUE YASUSHI (1907–91) was a poet and journalist, but he is best remembered in Japan for his historical novels, many of which have to do with China or Chinese-Japanese relations. Many of these works describe the ways that individuals are caught up in the grand movements of history and subjected to the workings of fate. This historical story, which describes a nineteenth-century expedition to the mountainous, rugged regions of northern Honshū, also deals with a similar theme. The story was first published in 1961.

on to Yonezawa. Now that the railroad has gone through, the highway has been largely abandoned. But in the last years of the nineteenth century, in fact, on July 13, 1888, when I set out from Kitakata to make the journey over the mountains, the road was rather crowded. Horses and travelers were commonplace because of the many sawmills around Hibara, which cut wood that was then hauled to Wakamatsu for use in the lacquer trade. The number of freight wagons carrying logs for that purpose alone was increasing daily, it seemed to me.

Though traveling on official business, we were not in a hurry, and from the very outset our excursion had a festive, holiday air about it. At the time I was working as a tax collector. Of course everyone supposes a tax collector is someone who goes around extorting money from poor people, but that was not really the case. Today we would call someone with my job a tax assessor or a surveyor of crop production.

Ours was the county office responsible for collecting taxes, and every year we were required to survey the amount of land under cultivation by the villages within our jurisdiction and to assess taxes on any land that had been cultivated since the previous year. Making that assessment was my job . . . but perhaps first I should explain that the town called Kitakata did not yet really exist. Instead, there were only the villages of Odatsuki and Koarai, which were separated by the Tazuki River; I worked for the county office located in Odatsuki. Back then the work we did was called "land production surveying." On the trip I am describing, our purpose was to survey the north flank of Mt. Bandai, which fell within the administrative district of Hibara village. My job was to survey the land that was being farmed by the many tiny villages scattered about the region popularly known as the "back side" of Mt. Bandai.

I was accompanied on the journey by two assistants, Tomekichi and Kinji. Tomekichi was of an age where his hair was beginning to be flecked with white. He was in his late forties, thin, and very serious. He walked with his kimono tucked up behind to allow greater freedom of movement. His spindly legs gave the impression that he was a pretty weak traveler, but in reality none of the rest of us could match him when it came to trekking through this wild north country. Kinji was a reticent young man of thirty who tended to be rather gloomy. He also wore his kimono tucked up and straw sandals on his feet. I was the only one of the group dressed anything like a modern tax assessor. I had dark blue work pants and a windbreaker, but like the others I wore straw sandals and had an extra pair tied to my belt.

Although I was the leader of the group, at age twenty-eight I was also the youngest. From the time I was twenty I had worked as a customs inspector for foreigners in Yokohama, so I had some knowledge and experience in the work of assessment; which is probably why, even at my age, I had become a person of authority in this rural county office. Tomekichi was not a professional assessor; he had originally come to the county office as a part-time employee, but over the years he had helped with the business of assessment and eventually joined the staff of the assessor's office. I believe he felt quite satisfied with the position he occupied. Kinji was a clerk who had only recently been employed in the Kitakata office. His handwriting was very neat and clear.

Our trips were usually scheduled to last ten days and we always made certain we had plenty of spare time. On our first day we planned to follow the familiar route from Kitakata to Hibara, and since it would hardly impress the villagers if we arrived in Hibara too early in the day and just lazed around, we made a point of loitering at tea shops along the road, and even paused for a nap under the shade of the trees once we reached the pass. Our clerk Kinji, who had only been married for about a month, dozed every time we stopped to rest, and was teased endlessly by Tomekichi.

The weather grew very warm and sweat bathed our bodies the moment we started walking, but whenever we paused to rest, the dry wind on our skin felt refreshingly cool. This was indeed the best time of the year to be traveling in this part of the country. The rainy season had been late and it was early July before we had any days that were completely cloudless. The weather was quite unusual that year and some people were concerned about the effect this would have on the crops. Since the weather had only just cleared, we had been accustomed to seeing a dull, overcast sky for days on end. But now the vital, green vegetation covering the mountains, the clean air that settled the dust, and the cloudless, deep, translucent blue sky all greeted us as we set out on our trip. We looked forward eagerly to days of pleasant traveling.

On that first day we finally arrived in Hibara around four o'clock. On the way, there was an incident so trivial it is probably not worth mentioning, except that I had reason to remember it afterward. We were walking along the bank of the Hibara River after coming down from Ōshio Pass when we met a woman going in the opposite direction, a woman dressed as a pilgrim making the rounds of the Sixty-six Holy Sites. For a moment she stood in silence blocking our way, until we saw that she appeared to be try-ing to say something. We clustered around, peering in-tently at her face and trying to catch her murmured words. She was muttering some sort of warning to us, saying "Go back. Go back. You will be in danger if you go any further." The woman appeared to be about forty and was dressed in the gray clothing typical of a pilgrim. A gray knapsack was on her back and she wore leggings and mittens to match. In one hand she carried a small bell. Her complexion was dark and made even darker by the liver spots of advancing age. She seemed to be a strong-willed and ill-tempered woman. She gazed steadily at us when she spoke, and I noticed that her eyes glittered with an unnatural bright-ness. She was no ordinary person.

Kinji and I both pushed past the woman, ignoring her words, but when Tomekichi tried to follow, she moved left or right several times, blocking his way, until finally he had no choice but to shove her aside. Having done that, he hurried to catch up with Kinji and myself, muttering, "Crazy woman! How unpleasant!" Nevertheless, Tome-kichi seemed to have been disturbed by what the woman said, for as we walked along he turned back two or three times to look in her direction, and seeing that she was still watching us, he murmured something about this en-counter being a very unlucky sign.

So, this was one of our experiences, but we were on the first day of our trip and were relieved at not having to face the drudgery of our usual office duties, and our spirits remained high. Later that day we felt several mild earthquake tremors. Once a jolt came just as we were crossing a bridge. It was not a suspension bridge, but the support beams began to creak, and we could see cracks appearing where the boards joined together. "It's an earthquake," said Tomekichi, and even before he spoke, I knew it was a strong one. Over the course of the previous month we had become quite familiar with earthquakes. Even in the region around Kitakata it was common to have two or three tremors a day that were sharp enough for a person to feel, so we had grown used to them and saw no cause for alarm.

Thinking about it later, it occurred to me that the warning the mad pilgrim woman had given us should not have been laughed off. Indeed, if we had listened to her and turned back at that point, most likely we would each be leading our appointed lives without ever having experienced the tragedy and sadness that soon befell us. When you come right down to it, man's intellect is a pretty shallow thing, and we never know what the future holds. So, as it turned out, we continued on our way, taking ourselves step by step unwittingly toward the gates of Hell.

Hibara, as I said earlier, was a village of some fifty houses located along the Yonezawa Highway. In earlier times it had been called Hinoki Yachi. The village was surrounded by groves of cypress called *hinoki*, so the original name of the place meant "valley choked with *hinoki*." The village lay in the shadow of Mt. Bandai, to the west of Mt. Azuma, and on the flank of Mt. Takasone. It was surrounded by mountains, and not only was there very little level ground in the region, hardly any of what was level had been brought under cultivation. In that sense, it was not a productive area. The people of the villages there preferred to make their living cutting wood or stripping bark for use in making paper, or by driving their packhorses over the mountains.

There were three inns in the village. Were one to continue along the road from Kitakata directly northeast and cross the pass at the county border, in another seven miles one would reach the village of Tsunagi; and from there it was another seven miles or more to Yonezawa. Hibara was indeed a tiny mountain settlement, but it was situated on a corridor used, much more then than at present, to spread the new Meiji enlightenment, and just four or five years earlier a troupe of Sumō wrestlers had passed through this region on their way to Yonezawa and Yamagata. We went guided by the village headman to the entry hall of an inn where we removed our traveling sandals. I noticed the inn sported an enormous sign announcing that it was here that the Sumō tour had stayed. Apparently the sign had been made soon after the wrestlers' visit.

It was our plan on the following morning to leave the Yonezawa Highway on which Hibara was located. We were to turn due south and follow the Nagase River through the forests that covered the lower slopes of Mt. Bandai. About four miles from Hibara was a hamlet of seven houses called Hosono, and a couple of miles further on was the village of Ōsawa, consisting of some twenty houses. At Ōsawa one stood directly beneath Bandai. It was only a couple of miles from Ōsawa to the hot spring resorts of Nakanoyu and Kaminoyu, located midway up the slope of Mt. Bandai; the road went straight up the side of the mountain. Several miles from Ōsawa toward the northeast flank of Bandai stood the village of Akimoto, which was composed of twelve households.

Our job on this trip was to survey these three villages—Hosono, Ōsawa, and Akimoto. We had postponed our survey in Hibara, thinking that since there was a village headman living there, we could conduct it any time. We decided to survey the three small villages buried deep in the mountain forests during the brief period between the end of the rainy season and the onset of really hot weather in midsummer.

That night, by previous arrangement, we had a meeting at our Hibara inn with the people from the village headman's office. We received support for our plan from the three members of the headman's staff, namely, Shuntarō, Kume, and Shinshū. Shinshū, of course, is an odd name, but everyone kept calling him "Shinshū, Shinshū," and soon I was following their example. Both Shuntarō and Kume were men in their sixties. Shuntarō was a rather reserved, aristocratic man, with large ears and a cheerful expression. Kume was quite the opposite, being somewhat impulsive and loud by nature. He had sunken eyes and prominent cheekbones. Shinshū was a small, intelligent man who managed all the details of the office work with a voluble tongue and vivid gestures. It was difficult to judge his age from his features; he might have been in his thirties or forties.

These three men were eager to have the land survey carried out and agreed to accompany us to the actual survey sites. Barely twenty years had passed since the Meiji Restoration and many local citizens thought we were try-

ing to cheat them when we described the system of levy-
ing land taxes. And so we had to marshal a force of workers at least this large to persuade a mere forty households
to consent to the annual survey.

Early the following morning, July 14, the six of us were
ready to depart. The three local men, Shuntarō, Kume, and
Shinshū, had the skirts of their kimonos tucked up like
Tomekichi and Kinji. We all wore leggings and straw sandals and used towels to protect our faces from the sun. Just
as we had all assembled in the earthen-floored hallway of
the inn to set out on our journey, we felt the first earthquake of the day. This was the most severe of the many
tremors we had experienced recently, and all of our group
as well as the maids at the inn quickly spilled out into the
road.

As we were leaving the village, we came to a bridge and
from there proceeded along the left bank of the Nagase.
Here the road curved gently in a southerly direction and
passed through an open area of stony ground. No sooner
had we come to that rocky place than we felt another
tremor. This one was milder than before and we supposed
it was merely an aftershock of the previous jolt. None of
our party made any comment, but it did give us reason to
pause. I noticed that the ground was littered with small
stones and the morning sunlight touched these stones,
glinting off the blades of grass that grew between them.
Even though it was still early, the sunlight sent up shimmering heat waves which promised a hot day ahead. To be
watching something as insubstantial as this haze of heat
and at the same moment to feel the ground begin to tremble filled me with uneasiness, as though even the earth

itself were not to be relied upon. But the tremor passed in an instant, like the shadow of a bird sweeping over the ground, and though an ominous feeling flickered through my mind, as soon as the trembling stopped I forgot all about it.

After leaving the flat land along the river we found ourselves confronted by the three massive peaks of Daibandai, Kobandai, and Akahani. Gazing at these lofty summits, we were deeply impressed by their grandeur. I had often heard people speak of the beauty of this region in the shadow of Mt. Bandai, and I now realized that it was in fact more magnificent than I had been told. From the lower slopes of the great mountain down to the river plain stretched large natural forests of cypress, oak, zelkova, and maple, which gave a dark, almost gloomy aspect to the landscape. The slopes of Bandai itself were covered with stands of red pine, white birch, and other sorts of trees. From where we stood on the riverbank the whole view was one vast wooded panorama. It was hard to believe that the three villages we planned to visit were somewhere out there beneath that sea of living trees. Indeed, it was a bit frightening to think that people spent their whole lives beneath the canopy of that seemingly endless forest.

Just before reaching Hosono, the road forked. One branch went along the lower slopes of Mt. Naka Azuma, and the other, the road we would follow, led in the direction of Mt. Bandai. We took the fork to the right and soon came to a long, log bridge that crossed over to the right bank of the Nagase River.

As we passed over the bridge, the clerk, Shinshū, noticed a swarm of toads moving beside the river.

"Look at all the toads down there among the stones. They must be migrating." Shinshū's comment prompted the rest of us to notice that what appeared to be stones beside the river was in fact a vast army of toads on the move. They followed one leap with another without a moment's pause, and since the ones behind kept surging forward, those in front had no choice but to keep moving. There was an odd single-mindedness in this moving, living mass. I had the feeling they were all intent on a single goal, allowing nothing to divert their attention.

We all commented on this remarkable sight and stood for a time entranced by it. Shinshū said that in the spring when the snow begins to melt he had seen groups of toads mating, but this was the first time he had ever seen so many of them migrating. Kume replied that once, about ten years ago, he had seen toads fighting in this area. Apparently one group had a dispute with another group from further up the river, and they had waged a toad battle to settle the issue by force. He was sure that was what these were up to as well.

"Come on! Let's get going. We'll never get our survey done if we just stand here," said Tomekichi. At this the rest of us turned away from the toads and continued on our way.

Around ten o'clock we reached the village of Hosono. I call it a village though it consisted of no more than seven households. They were nice, sturdy houses clustered together on a narrow piece of land closed in on the east and west by the peaks of Hachimori and Tsurugigamine. The encroaching hills seemed to crowd into the village on both sides. This was truly a mountain hamlet. The main work of the men there was logging, and each of the houses had a small shed attached which looked something like a chicken coop. Here the family kept a wood lathe or two. The farming was left to the women, and when we arrived at the village there was no sign of them because they were all out in the fields.

Tomekichi was taken by one of the villagers to the mountains behind the settlement so that he could get a view of the layout of the fields, while the rest of us passed the time in desultory conversation with an old man who had once been a logger. There was another small tremor during our talk.

While waiting for Tomekichi to return, we met some of the men of the village and made preliminary arrangements for the survey we would be conducting during the next few days. Having accomplished that much, we left Hosono and headed on. Beyond the village the land suddenly opened out into low, rolling hills. A broad plain spread east and west, and standing in the middle of it we had an unobstructed view of Mt. Bandai.

After leaving Hosono our route turned away from the river we had been following for so long. Ōsawa was a couple of miles further along this road, which ran through virgin forests. Actually the path was so narrow it could hardly be called a road. We passed places called Kiyomogihara and Ōfuchi, but they were merely names, for we did not see a single dwelling. At Kiyomogihara we met a group of people, including some women, who were coming down from one of the hot spring resorts on Mt. Bandai. The group consisted of a man and his wife who were in their fifties, their youngest son who was fifteen or sixteen, the wife's younger sister who was in her thirties, and two young men from the village of Shiobara near Hibara who were serving as guides to the group.

The man was a merchant from the Niigata region who had gone to the resort of Nakanoyu for a month's treatment, but they had cut short their visit by a full week and were now hurrying down the mountain, having formed the uneasy impression that the mountains were somehow different from usual.

The husband had the sallow complexion one associates with the chronically ill, and he remained silent in a sullen, bad humor. The woman's face was tight with emotional strain of the sort seen in hysterical people, and she rattled on like a person unable to stop talking. According to her story, four or five days earlier they had been surprised to find that the amount of hot mineral water flowing down from Kaminoyu had dropped off significantly. Also, the quantity of steam that issued from among the rocks had inexplicably increased in both volume and pressure. Although Nakanoyu still had plenty of water for the baths, in the past couple of days it had become so hot no one could bathe in it. In addition, the mountain had been rumbling for the past four or five days and the rumbling had grown more ominous each day. This morning the sound was so fierce it seemed the mountain itself might burst. Then, of course, there had been the tremors. The woman said they made a habit of coming to this resort every year, but this was the first time anything strange had occurred, and they thought something alarming was going to happen.

In concluding their story the wife said, "There are many other people besides ourselves who are frightened and leaving the mountain. And now we meet a group like yourselves going in the opposite direction. I suppose it takes all kinds." She estimated that there were still some thirty guests at the Kaminoyu hot spring and about twenty each at Nakanoyu and Shimonoyu.

One of the young guides from Shiobara said that for the past ten years people had often predicted that Mt. Bandai was about to blow its top, but it never had. Still, given the recent events, he thought it might blow this year after all. Last night there had been a light sprinkling of rain on the mountain, but today on the way down he had noticed that the small lake at Numanotaira had completely dried up. His view was that this sort of thing could be a frightening sign if one chose to interpret it that way, and yet it might not mean anything at all. On Mt. Bandai he felt that such signs were cause for alarm. The young man explained all this to us falteringly in the local dialect. Judging from what he said, he might have had reason to be worried, and then again, maybe not. But his fear was evident in the inconclusive way he spoke. He finished by saying, "What can one do, anyway?" Motioning for the rest of the group to follow, he led them quickly down the mountain. The young man had used the odd phrase, "blow its top," suggesting that it might erupt, but in the local dialect this literally meant that the whole top of the mountain would blow off.

We were a bit disturbed by these stories from the family from Niigata, but we did not feel all that uneasy about getting any closer to the mountain they were fleeing. After parting with the merchant and his family, the normally reserved Shuntarō said, "In all my life I have never seen so many snakes as we've seen today. I, too, believe something odd is going on." I had also noticed the snakes, but since this was my first trip to the area, I thought perhaps this was just a place where they were unusually common. After leaving Hosono we saw any number of them crossing the road with their heads raised. Every time we stopped to rest and looked around before sitting down, we saw something long and thin slither off silently into the bushes. The fact that Shuntarō, a local resident and a man not much given to expressing his opinions, commented on the matter seemed to be all the more significant. Then, in response, Kume tilted his head to one side and said, "I haven't been aware of the snakes particularly, but I have noticed that the doves and pheasants seem upset. I've hunted for years, but I've never seen birds as worked up as this." Kinji, who had hardly said a word all day, had a frightened look on his face, and in ominous tones said, "Yesterday, we met that pilgrim just below the pass. Do you remember what she said?" He turned to Kume as he spoke.

At the same moment, from the other side Tomekichi said, "Kinji!" ordering him to be quiet in a surprisingly harsh tone of voice. "Don't talk about that rubbish!" This outburst was strange coming from the usually taciturn Tomekichi.

Shinshū was the only one in the group who appeared to be totally unaffected by the atmosphere of tension that had developed. "Sometimes the mountains rumble and the snakes and birds move about. What's wrong with that? If you start letting yourself get excited about every little thing you'll have another stroke, Shuntarō. And you, Kume, to hear you talk, one would think you're getting senile as well as bald." He made a joke of the situation, but what he said had been instructive as well. I realized for the first time that

Shuntarō's usually phlegmatic attitude toward things was due to the fact that he had once had a stroke. As for Kume, I had thought he kept his head shaved, but after Shinshū commented on his baldness, I noticed that in fact he had small wisps of hair growing here and there on his head.

It was one o'clock when we arrived in Ōsawa. The village was composed of several parts with names such as Oshisawa, Osusawa, and so on, and there was no way of knowing for sure which was the original name. Various people had from time to time made different entries in the county register, calling the place by different names. I suppose it didn't much matter what its real name was, since everyone within the boundaries of the forest, whether they lived in the village itself or elsewhere, referred to it simply as Ōsawa. There were twenty houses and some two hundred people living there. They had a splendid view of Mt. Bandai from dawn to dusk.

We asked the people there to provide us with lodging for the night, and then, since the sun was still high in the sky, we set out for Akimoto, which was a couple of miles further on to the northeast. We had planned to begin our survey there the following morning, so we wanted to have a look at the site today and talk a bit with its inhabitants. Just beyond Ōsawa the Nagase River turned sharply east, making a wide sweep around the base of Mt. Bandai. As everyone knows, this is the river that flows into Lake Inawashiro on the front side of Mt. Bandai. In the area where we found ourselves, the river was flanked on both sides by broad, flat plains. After leaving Ōsawa we followed a road upstream along the river. About a mile from the village we came to the spot where the Ono joined the Nagase. From that point onward, the Nagase became a wide stretch of water. Another mile further on was the confluence of the Ogura. Akimoto consisted of a dozen houses located several hundred yards from where the two rivers ran together.

The lower slopes of Mt. Bandai between Ōsawa and Akimoto were carpeted with thick forests broken occasionally by high meadows and rolling hills. A clump of white birch crowned one hill, and here and there were broad open spaces overgrown with dwarf bamboo and reeds taller than a man. These open, brushy spaces created striped patterns across the flank of the mountain.

As we traveled from Hosono to Ōsawa, the peak known as Kobandai was directly in front of us, while on the right and left were Akahani and Daibandai. These three together formed the massif known collectively as Mt. Bandai. The peaks had towered before us for a long while, but when we reached the village of Akimoto, the view of Mt. Bandai had assumed a new aspect. Up until then Kushigamine, which was actually some distance to the left, seemed quite close to the three peaks of Bandai and appeared to be a fourth in the group, but from Akimoto we could see that there was a considerable distance separating them, and that Bandai was a different mountain entirely. It was, at any rate, a beautiful view.

At Akimoto we were served tea at one of the farmhouses, and while enjoying this new view of Mt. Bandai we made arrangements with the local people to begin our survey the following morning. As we sat together on the long veranda of the house discussing these matters, we felt the jolt of yet another earthquake. The old farmer who owned the house thought it was perfectly natural that the people of Ōsawa were upset by so many earthquakes. He suggested that we would be safer if we finished our work in Ōsawa as quickly as possible and came here to his village.

It was from this farmer that we learned for the first time that the wells of Ōsawa had gone dry and that the tremors had been especially sharp there, with the rumbling of the mountain reaching unusual proportions. The people of Ōsawa had been living in constant fear, and had not been able to work in their fields for the past ten days, wondering among themselves whether they should evacuate their homes or not.

Akimoto and Ōsawa were both in the shadow of Mt. Bandai, but there were several long swales running north of the mountain in such a way that they set Ōsawa apart. It was a common belief that whenever anything strange happened on the mountain, Ōsawa alone felt the effect of it. The people of Akimoto were quite unconcerned, treating Ōsawa's misfortunes as though they were standing on one bank of a river watching a city burn on the opposite shore.

When we heard all this, we did not feel much like spending the night at Ōsawa, and wondered how the people there must feel at having to provide hospitality for us while they themselves were frightened for their lives. Still, we had already asked them to arrange lodging for us for that night, and the following day we would be free to make other plans, so with this in mind we decided to return.

On reaching the place where the Nagase and Ono rivers met, we came across a young man and woman dressed much

more fashionably than other people in the region. Even seeing them from afar we could not imagine they were locals,
and since we were walking at a faster pace we soon overtook the pair. They were probably in their early twenties and
everything about them suggested the sophistication of city-
dwellers. At first glance the man appeared to be a student
of some sort; he was wearing casual Western clothing and
carrying a Western-style umbrella. The woman had a pale
complexion and a round, feminine face. Her head was covered by a shawl, and judging from her hairstyle and elegant,
striped kimono we could only suppose that she came from
a fashionable Tōkyō neighborhood.

When I asked the pair where they were heading, the
man mentioned the Kaminoyu hot spring, but the only
luggage they had was a single cloth-wrapped bundle which
the woman carried. Although they were obviously travelers, it seemed unlikely that they were typical guests at a
local spa. Shinshū asked when they expected to reach
Kaminoyu, yet neither of them could reply. In fact, they did
not know where exactly Kaminoyu was, or which road to
take, or how far it would be; they seemed to be just strolling
casually about the fields and meadows on the lower slopes
of Mt. Bandai.

I all but insisted that they spend the night with us at
Ōsawa. Under the circumstances it appeared to be the only
solution, since they seemed almost in a daze. The woman
hesitated and looked as if she wanted the man to refuse,
but he seemed rather weak-willed and finally, as though
making a concession to me, he agreed to go with us.

The young couple was considerably slower than we

were, so I paused from time to time to let them catch up. As I waited I had occasion to inspect the woman. She was extraordinarily attractive. Though she was not strikingly beautiful in the traditional sense, there was a purity and innocence in her face, in the way she walked and in the smallest movement she made, that impressed me more deeply than any other woman I had seen.

Eventually we made our way back to Ōsawa along with our two new companions, and Shinshū had no trouble arranging accommodation for them as well. As it turned out, I stayed in one house with the young man and woman while the other five stayed across the road. The village well had dried up so we were not able to have a bath that night, but otherwise we were treated with remarkable hospitality by the people of the village.

As we had learned in Akimoto, the people here were frightened by the earthquakes and the rumbling of the mountain and were all ready to flee, but our hosts seemed to take courage from our presence and from having additional people to share the house with them.

Both the house where I was lodged and the one where Tomekichi and the others stayed were occupied by large extended families which included people of several generations. Not just in Ōsawa, but in Hosono and Akimoto as well, there were many households with large numbers of children; apparently eight or nine per family was normal around here.

All the homes were built in the same pattern, having a large room with a sunken hearth and wooden floor that faced a dirt-floored hallway. Beyond the room with the hearth was a smaller living room, and beyond that a wooden door which led to a back room. The living room looked out on the front garden, and the back room faced the rear gate; both were bordered by a small veranda. It was decided that I would sleep in the living room, the young couple would have the back room, and all the members of the large family would sleep together in the room with the wooden floor and sunken hearth.

After it was decided who would sleep where, the young couple and I joined the rest of the family around the hearth where we were served dinner. As we ate, the farmer and his wife told us of several unusual happenings. This year's snow had been deeper than usual but had melted off early, and recently the people from Tsuchida had gone into the swamp to cut walnut trees. They had heard a loud report like the sound of a tree trunk snapping, but it had come from deep within the earth so the people had been frightened and had run away. Also, at about nine o'clock in the evening on April 15, a pale blue flame had flared from the peak of Mt. Bandai and flashed across the sky, followed a few moments later by a great rumbling sound. As the parents related these stories, the children sat in a cluster gazing intently at their faces, and whenever I interrupted with a comment, they all turned in unison to stare at me. I noticed that the young man and woman hardly said a word all evening, and they seemed so preoccupied with their own thoughts I was worried about them. They replied in monosyllables when spoken to, but they never initiated a conversation.

As we were eating dinner, another guest arrived at the house. He told us he had set out from Hibara at about noon that day. Sitting on the edge of the raised floor by the hallway unlacing his straw sandals, he spoke with great animation, saying this was the first time he had made the trip from Hibara and that he had found the road bad and it had been farther than he thought, and that altogether he had had a rough time of it. He was completely uninhibited as he talked on and on. When at last he approached the hearth where the rest of us were seated and the light of the lamp fell on his face, he appeared to be a salesman of some sort, about forty years old, with surprisingly pleasant features.

Somehow we all knew right away that he would end up telling us the story of his life even though no one asked to hear it. He said he came from a certain village on the front side of Mt. Bandai. As a young man he had left home and gone to Ōsaka where he had been successful in the fishcake business. Over the years he had saved a little money, and now for the first time he was on his way back to his village for a visit. He planned to sponsor an elaborate memorial service for his parents who were now dead, but his real purpose in returning to his birthplace was to surprise the people there, and to watch their mouths drop open in amazement when they saw how successful he had been.

Since his home was on the other side of Mt. Bandai, the normal route would have been by way of Inawashiro, which was closer and easier. But he was not taking the usual road, and indeed the fact that he had decided to approach the mountain by way of Hibara and make a surprise return to his village seemed typical of a small-time entrepreneur who had achieved some measure of success.

He was clearly easy prey to flattery and somewhat proud and boastful, but hardly to the point of being disagreeable. There was also a good side to his nature, and I found it admirable that he had been thrifty and industrious enough to save some of his money for this trip.

Until this man's arrival the people of the household had told us only the most gloomy and discouraging stories about Mt. Bandai, but once this lively character appeared, the tone of the conversation changed completely. From that point on sounds of laughter burst out time and again from the group gathered around the hearth. And yet even while we were talking we felt one slight tremor and heard the mountain rumble twice. The tremor was very mild, but it filled our hearts with dread nonetheless, and the small children clung desperately to their parents with frightened faces and began to cry. The other sounds I took merely to be the wind, and when I learned they came from the mountain, I realized that I had already heard them several times that day. The rumbling of the mountain was quite different from the earthquake tremors in that the children neither cried nor clung to their parents. Rather, I thought I could detect signs of extraordinary intensity in their innocent faces as they strained to follow the sound as it died away somewhere deep within the earth. It seemed cruel that these youngsters had to endure such dread and anxiety.

That night, after we had finished dinner, all of us including the family members retired to bed early. The fish-cake merchant from Ōsaka ended up sleeping in the living room with me and we arranged our quilts side by side. No sooner had his head touched his pillow than he was sound asleep and snoring loudly.

I also was soon asleep, but I slept lightly and was awakened a short time later. The moment my eyes opened I heard the faint noise of the shutters being slid open in the back room. The sound lasted only a moment, then stopped, but after a brief silence it was repeated. I had an idea that these cautious noises had been going on for some time. I strained my ears trying to hear what was happening in the back room and presently I heard footsteps and the rustle of clothing. Judging from the sounds, I determined that the young couple was leaving the house by way of the veranda. Somehow, ever since going to bed I had a feeling that something like this might happen, and I realized why I had been sleeping so lightly. In any case, now that I was aware of what was going on, I knew I could not simply ignore the situation.

Without hesitation I threw open the shutters of the living room and stepped down into the garden in my bare feet. The moonlight made the scene outside as bright as midday. I could clearly make out the leaves of the nandina bushes at the bottom of the garden. I went around the side of the house to the back and followed a path that passed beside the well and came out in a corner of a field that was terraced up one level higher than the garden. The wild plants and the tassels of the pampas grass shone silver in the moonlight, stretching away into the distance. Far across the field I could make out the figures of the young couple as they walked away from the farmhouse.

The situation did not seem critical enough to require

that I dash after them, so I merely quickened my pace and began to catch up. When I got within fifty yards of them they turned around and I called out, "Don't be fools! Where do you think you're going?" I tried to make my voice sound as loud and peremptory as possible. The woman looked as if she was ready to break into a panicky run, but quickly gave up with a slump of resignation. She hid her face behind her sleeve and began to weep. The young man seemed utterly incapable of doing anything, and from the moment I called out, he just stood there dazed.

The woman was dressed in a different kimono from the one she had worn earlier. It was of a deep purple fabric, and in the brilliant moonlight her pale face contrasted sharply with its color. I had a suspicion that she had death in mind when she put on her finest clothes.

Her face was tear-stained as she looked up and said, "Neither of us is prepared to go on living." I ignored her and merely told them to go back to the house, setting out in that direction myself. When we reached the well at the rear I stopped to wash my feet. They both followed my example and washed theirs too. Since I had no shoes to put on, I entered the house through the back room and from there returned to my own bed in the living room. For a while I heard the woman softly sobbing, but I paid no attention to this and was soon asleep.

The following day, July 15, I was woken by a loud rumbling in the earth. It was shortly before six o'clock. I knew the time because the fish-cake merchant also rose from his bed at the same moment. From somewhere on his person he produced an enormous gold pocket watch, and holding it up to a ray of bright sunlight that had slipped through a crack in the shutters, he announced the time.

Since neither of us could get back to sleep again, we opened the shutters and seated ourselves on the veranda, where we each smoked a cigarette and felt the cool morning air on our skin. As we sat there, we heard the shutters of the back room and the room where the family had slept being opened. Apparently everyone had been woken by the sound of the mountain, though of course this was not such an early hour for a farming family to be getting up. It looked as though the people in the house across the road had been awake for some time. I saw Tomekichi and Shuntarō in the front garden discussing something as they laced up their traveling sandals. Moments later Kume, Kinji, and Shinshū also appeared; they were getting ready to start the survey. Since I still had to eat breakfast I decided to delay my departure and set off a little behind them.

I was watching their movements without really paying much attention when Tomekichi happened to look over in our direction. Apparently he caught sight of me, for he waved. He gestured to indicate that they would go on ahead, and I watched as they set out from the garden and disappeared from sight: Kume, Shuntarō, Tomekichi, Shinshū, and Kinji, in that order.

About thirty minutes after the others had left the house across the road, I started after them with the fish-cake merchant and the young couple. The woman was dressed in the same purple kimono she had worn the night before, which led me to suspect that they had not yet given up the idea of taking their lives; the thought irritated me.

"I'm going on to Akimoto from here," I said to the couple. "You had better come with me. I can find someone there to accompany you as far as Inawashiro."

The man nodded slightly in acknowledgment, but the woman kept her eyes on the ground and said nothing. From their expressions I had the feeling that the man had already abandoned the idea of suicide and that it was only the woman who was still determined to carry out their plan. Perhaps, I thought, the man had never really been interested in killing himself and had only been led unwillingly to these alpine meadows by his companion. If that were the case, the woman's desire to take her life seemed especially poignant.

We set out along the river, the same road I had taken to Akimoto the day before. Just as on the previous day, the sky was delightfully clear: a limpid, pale blue unmarred by clouds. A short distance out of the village of Ōsawa the road crossed a small stream flowing down from the Kobuka marsh. Just beyond the stream the road forked, one branch going to Akimoto and the other to Kawakami and Nagasaka.

There the merchant parted company with us and went off along the upward sloping road, half hidden by the scrub bamboo. All we could see of him was his white shirt, the cloth bundle in which he carried his spare clothes, and a small knapsack. He walked away from us with disagreeable swiftness, and soon even his white shirt was lost from sight.

Accompanied by the silent couple from the city I set off toward the confluence of the Ono River. After parting from the merchant, we had hardly gone any distance at all before we saw about ten children from the village standing on an outcrop at the top of a low hill that flanked our road. The youngest was perhaps five or six and the oldest about ten years old. Apparently they had come from the village looking for a place to play. There was certainly no school playground in such a remote village, and no doubt once these youngsters were a little older they would be busy doing chores around the house, but they were not yet old enough for that. It was just the height of the silk-making season, and to keep them from being underfoot, the younger ones were sent out every morning to play by themselves in the open fields.

They stood clustered together on the outcrop above and solemnly gazed at us as we passed along the road below. I looked up at them and wondered if any of them belonged to the family in whose home we had spent the night. All these farm children looked more or less the same to me; they were the same faces I had seen masked with fear as they sat around the hearth when the earthquake had struck, the same faces I had seen straining to hear the receding sound of the rumbling mountain. I could not distinguish the children of one family from those of another, but felt that if any of the group had been in our house, I would like to call out some word of greeting.

It was at that precise moment that everything happened. At exactly 7:40 the earth gave a great heave and shudder. This was different from the tremors we had felt before, much more violent, and I was knocked to the ground. I could not tell if it came from the mountain or the ground beneath me, but I heard the most terrifying sound issuing from the bowels of the earth. I saw the young woman lose her balance, stagger, and fall to her knees. I scrambled to my feet only to be thrown down again by a second violent jolt. This time I used my right arm to brace my body against the bucking earth. I glanced up at the outcrop to see if the children had also been thrown down, but there was no sign of them. All I could see was a swirl of dust slowly rising in the air.

By this time I knew better than to try and leap up again, but after the second quake subsided, I carefully rose to my feet. Beside me I saw that the young man had reached out a hand and was helping the woman up as well.

At the same moment, I saw two or three small heads poke up above the edge of the outcrop. Soon all the heads appeared in a row and I heard one of the children cry out in a loud voice, cadenced almost as though he were singing, "Blow, mountain, blow! Give it all you've got!" Soon several of the others joined in, shouting with all their tiny might, "Blow, mountain, blow! Give it all you've got!"

Their chant—or scream of defiance, whatever it was— was scarcely finished when in thunderous answer a roar came rolling back over the earth. It was a blast so powerful that I was lifted off my feet and hurled to the ground several yards to my right. On and on went the roar while the earth heaved in convulsive spasms. Later, when I tried to recall the exact sequence of events, I was never sure just when it was that I happened to catch sight of Mt. Bandai, but I know I saw a huge column of fire and smoke rising straight up into the clear tranquil sky; like one of the pillars of Hell it rose to twice the height of the mountain itself. The whole mountain had literally exploded and the shape of Kobandai was blotted out forever. It was only much later, of course, that I realized what had occurred.

I cannot say with any certainty how I survived the explosion. The entire north face of Mt. Bandai came avalanching down in a sea of sand, rocks, and boulders. I remember it now as a nightmare vision, as something so terrifying as to be not of this world. The avalanche obliterated the forests that covered the lower slopes of the mountain. The wall of debris swept down with terrible speed and force. I saw the purple kimono swirl up in the air like a scrap of colored paper, and in a flash it was swept away in that tide of mud. I do not know exactly where or when it was that the kimono disappeared from sight. The air was so thick with clouds of ash and pebbles I could not tell whether it was day or night. I staggered along the bank of the Ono River and sought refuge on the high ground north of Akimoto. That alone saved my life. If I had fled in any other direction I would simply have been whisked away without a trace.

Within an hour of the time Mt. Bandai exploded, the villages of Hosono, Ōsawa, and Akimoto were all swept away, and whatever remained was buried under yards and yards of stone. As most of my readers will know, it was not just the north slope that was affected; many villages on the east side of the mountain also met the same tragic fate.

Many accurate and detailed studies and reports have been published regarding the eruption of Mt. Bandai, and I certainly have nothing to add to them. My intention here has been quite different, for it was a personal experience of the eruption that I wanted to relate.

What remains indelibly burned upon my memory and ringing in my ears is the defiant challenge—"Blow, mountain, blow! Give it all you've got!"—uttered by those brave children, who could do nothing else in the face of the mountain's awesome power.

And one more thing: officially, 477 people died that day, but for the sake of accuracy I believe at least three more casualties should be added to that number. Although their names are not known, I feel that when we honor the victims of this disaster we must also mention the departed souls of that young man and woman and the fish-cake merchant from Ōsaka as well. Today Hosono, Ōsawa, and Hibara are all buried beneath the large lake that formed when the stones and mud of the eruption blocked the Nagase River. Akimoto lies at the bottom of another such lake. Though I have related this story in some detail, the fact is that I have never gone back to visit the area, and it is unlikely that I ever shall. The region today, they tell me, is noted for its pristine alpine lakes, but who can say what terrible memories would revive if I were to go there again and gaze upon them. No, I shall never revisit the countryside that lies in the shadow of Mt. Bandai.

Translated by Stephen W. Kohl

The City of Trees

Oda Sakunosuke

PEOPLE SAY ŌSAKA is a city with no trees, but when I think back to my childhood I find I have a remarkable number of memories that involve trees. There were the big old camphor trees in the grounds of the Ikutama Shrine that were supposed to have snakes living in them and that I consequently was afraid to go near. Or the gingko trees in the grounds of the Kitamuki Hachiman Shrine where I hung out my clothes to dry after I accidentally fell into the lotus pond there. And the old pines in the temple compounds in Nakadera-machi that were the same color as the cicadas that hid in their branches, or the trees that spread their green shade over the steep lanes of Genshō-ji Slope or Kuchinawa Slope. No, I wouldn't say I grew up in a city

ODA SAKUNOSUKE (1913–47) was a native of Ōsaka but spent his school years in Kyōto. In the early years of the Pacific War, Oda earned a name for himself writing with wit and unadorned realism about the people of his hometown. This elegiac evocation of the city Oda knew as a child appeared in print in March 1944, at the height of World War II. Just months afterward, American bombing raids destroyed much of Ōsaka, including the "High City" where Oda had spent his childhood.

without trees. As far as I am concerned, Ōsaka has lots of trees.

Try going up in one of the tall buildings in the Sennichi-mae area. If you look east toward the Kōzu bluff on the north and the Ikutama and Yūhigaoka bluffs that flank it on the south, you will see that, beyond the smoke and dust that smudge the air, there is still a mass of luxuriant green there, its depths peaceful and silent as they have been for countless centuries.

That is the area of Ōsaka popularly referred to as Uemachi, the High City. We who were born and raised in the High City always spoke of "going down below" when we went to the Semba, Shima-no-uchi or Sennichi-mae areas. But we did not think of the High City as being in contrast to the Shitamachi or Low City. The High City of Ōsaka is called that because it is situated on the bluffs, but the bluff area has none of the associations of elegance or elitism that go with the Yamanote or hilly region of Tōkyō. The communities on the Ōsaka bluffs grew up around the temples and shrines there, or on what was said to be the site of the Takatsu Palace, where Emperor Nintoku in ancient times wrote the poem that begins, "Ascending my high hall . . ."* Such communities prided themselves on the degree to which they preserved the quiet dignity associated with these traditions of the past, and indeed some-

---

*A poem preserved in *Shin kokinshū*, ch. 6, and attributed to Emperor Nintoku (r. 313–399), who had his capital at Naniwa, the old name for Ōsaka. The poem reads: "Ascending my high hall / I see the smoke rising— / the kitchens of my people / are bustling indeed!" The exact site of Takatsu Palace has never been determined, though several areas in the hilly section of Ōsaka lay claim to it. *(Trans.)*

thing of that atmosphere did cling to the areas. But there were other areas such as the main street in front of the Kōzu Shrine, the Babasaki area around Ikutama Shrine, or the Gataro Alley district in Nakadera-machi that as early as the Genroku era in the seventeenth century had become thoroughly imbued with that air of freedom and liveliness characteristic of the Ōsaka Low City. So even those of us who were born in the High City in a sense grew up as Low City children.

The High City had a lot of little alleys—which is to say there were a lot of poor people living there. At the same time there were lots of slopes and rises, which is natural enough since the area was situated on the bluff. When we spoke of "going down below" we meant going west down these slopes. Jizō Slope, Shōgen-ji Slope, Aizen Slope, Kuchinawa Slope—just saying the names brings back happy memories. Kuchinawa in particular has fond associations for me.

In Ōsaka dialect "kuchinawa" is another name for snake, and as one may have guessed, Kuchinawa Slope was so called because of the way the old flight of stone steps that went up the slope wriggled up and down like a snake as it threaded among the trees. If you had come right out and called it Snake Slope the whole effect would have been ruined, but by calling it Kuchinawa Slope you give it a feeling of quaintness and humor, and for that reason when I think of the slopes in Ōsaka, Kuchinawa is the first name that comes to mind.

When I was a boy, however, I took no interest in what kind of atmosphere was suggested by the name Kuchinawa Slope. Rather it was the name associated with the area at the top of the slope, Yūhigaoka or Evening Sun Hill, that attracted me and roused my curiosity. The name Yūhigaoka I'm sure dates back a long way. In the old times if you looked west from the bluff here you could no doubt have gotten a good view of the sun as it went down in Naniwa Bay. I think it was Fujiwara no Ietaka who wrote the poem that goes:

> Bound by karma,
> I've come to make my home
> in Naniwa village
> and to gaze in reverence
> at the setting sun on the waves.

Because he was living on the bluff at the time he wrote the poem, I guess it was inevitable that the place should come to be called Evening Sun Hill.

But to return to the subject of my childhood, at that time historical or literary matters such as these were no concern of mine. It was the fact that halfway up Kuchinawa Slope was the location of the Yūhigaoka Girls' School that set my impressionable young brain on fire. Even now I remember how for no particular reason I would stand at the top of the slope in the late afternoon watching the girls in their school uniforms as they came up the steps, and my face would flush with excitement as though colored by the evening sun.

At that time I was a student in a middle school situated on what was said to have been the site of the Takatsu Palace. After graduating from middle school, however, I entered a high school in Kyōto and the scene of my youthful activities shifted from Ōsaka to the Yoshida area of Kyōto. Thereafter, on the rare occasions when I came home on vacation from Kyōto, the sights of Ōsaka that had thrilled and delighted me when I was a little boy, such as the night stalls at Komagaike or Enoki, seemed as hopelessly drab and dull as faded wallpaper. And then while I was still attending high school in Kyōto both my parents died. That put a finish to our Ōsaka house, since there was no one left to live in it, and for all practical purposes my connections with the old Ōsaka neighborhood came to an end.

Alone in the world, I soon became accustomed to drifting from one lodging to another and forgot all about the place where I was born. Later I had occasion to write about the area in several of my stories, but always in a highly fictionalized manner, not describing it as it had actually been. And though I wrote about it, it never occurred to me to pay a visit to the place. That's how lazy I was.

In early spring of last year, however, something came up that made it necessary for me to stop by the local city office in the ward of Ōsaka where I was born and am legally registered. And in order to get to the ward office I had to go through my old neighborhood. Here was a chance to have a look at the place for the first time in ten years, I thought to myself with excitement. And when I began considering what route to take, my feet just naturally turned in the direction of Kuchinawa Slope.

Along the way I noted that the Yūhigaoka Girls' School had moved elsewhere; the entrance to the school was now marked by a sign that read PRIVATE SCHOOL FOR BOYS. Just once, when I was a middle-school student, I had had an opportunity to pass through the entrance, ordinarily so totally off-limits to me.

At that time the Yūhigaoka Girls' School had set up a basketball division and had requested that some of the outstanding players from our school be sent over to coach their students. It was the kind of relaxed thing people did in those days—sending a bunch of boys over to a girls' school. Our school, I might explain, held as prominent a place in the field of student basketball as Wakayama Middle School did in the field of secondary-school baseball. I had just signed up for the basketball division four days earlier, but I brazenly tagged along in the wake of the experts and in this way got to pass through the gate of Yūhigaoka Girls' School.

It turned out, however, that among the students we were supposed to coach was a very pretty girl named Mizuhara whom I happened to know, though she didn't know me, and this threw me into a panic. Inevitably, she had an opportunity to observe that I, who was supposed to be one of the leading players, was actually clumsier at handling the ball than the girls we had been sent to coach, and no doubt she despised me for it. Anyway, after that I gave up basketball and never again had occasion to pass through the gate of the girls' school. All this came into my mind as I walked up the slope.

At the top of the slope was an alley. Once you emerged from the alley, you could turn south and go toward Shitennō-ji temple, or north to Ikutama Shrine. The streets connecting the temple and shrine areas were musty with the odor of the past, as symbolized in the almost perversely plain sign that hung in front of the sculptor of Buddhist images, a board carved in bas-relief with the single word ARTIST. Looking around me for the first time in ten years, I realized how uncannily few changes the neighborhood had undergone. Turning north along the shady street that ran in the direction of Gataro Alley, I could see to my delight the same old temples and houses and trees that had been there in the past. Only the eaves of the houses were much lower than I had remembered, and this made it seem as though I were walking through a strange area. Then it dawned on me that this was because I was now quite a different height from what I had been ten years ago.

Next to the *geta* store was the drugstore, and next to the drugstore was the public bath. Next to the public bath was the barbershop. Next to the barbershop was the store selling Buddhist articles. Next to the store selling Buddhist articles was the man who makes tubs and pails. Next to the man who makes tubs and pails was the man who makes nameplates. And next to the man who makes nameplates was—my goodness! The bookstore was gone!

It was called Zenshodō, Hall of Good Books. When I was young I was an avid reader of juvenile magazines such as *Young People's Club* and *Anthill*, and also an avid contributor to their readers' columns. Whenever it was about time for a new issue to appear, I would make two or three trips daily to the bookstore to see if any of the funny stories I had submitted had by chance come out in print. Zenshodō also carried secondhand books and books for lending, and they had the Tachikawa paperback series as well. I was a sixth grader at the time and immersed in reading things like Kunikida Doppo's *An Honest Man*, Morita Sōhei's *Smoke*, and Arishima Takeo's *The Descendants of Cain*. In fact I spent so much time browsing around the shelves of Zenshodō that I almost didn't get into middle school.

But now Zenshodō was gone. The owner had been a man with a big nose. I remember that whenever I would bring in secondhand books and ask if he would buy them, the size of his nose for some reason troubled me greatly. I stood in front of what had once been Zenshodō and gazed up at the sign hanging in its entrance, which said Yano Music Store. As I did so, the old man in the nameplate store paused in the middle of painting a name and stared intently in my direction, just as he used to do decades ago.

I remembered his face because it had so many warts on it, and I started to go toward him, thinking I would speak to him. But he took no notice of me and instead, after removing his glasses, disappeared into the rear of the store. Feeling somewhat rebuffed, I decided to have a look inside Yano Music Store. There was still a little time before I had to be at the ward office.

It was quite dark inside the store. Coming in from the bright noonday light of the street, I peered around in confusion, trying to get my bearings. The only things I could make out clearly were a death mask of Beethoven and a ship's life preserver, both of which hung on the wall and stood out immediately because of their white color. It appeared that the store specialized in buying, selling, and swapping high-quality phonograph records, and I thought it rather peculiar that it should have a life preserver hanging on the wall. But then my attention turned to the proprietor of the store, who by this time had made his appearance. At first I couldn't see his face very distinctly, but as my eyes became adjusted to the dim light, I thought with a start that I had surely seen him somewhere before, though I couldn't recall where.

His nose was not very large—certainly nothing like that of the proprietor of Zenshodō. But he had thick lips that he smacked together when he talked, like a goldfish gobbling food. I was suddenly reminded of the professional storyteller Tokugawa Musei. At the same time I wondered if perhaps I hadn't seem him somewhere at a public bath, sitting in the booth at the entrance collecting bath fees. He seemed to be over fifty. No matter how I looked at him, though, I couldn't picture him as the kind of man who ran a fancy store selling records of Western music. And for that matter, the store itself didn't seem like the kind that belonged in this neighborhood.

Here I was passing through my old district in the middle of the day on my way to the city office—it was hardly an appropriate time to become engrossed in listening to phonograph records. On the other hand, I didn't particularly feel like confronting the proprietor and plying him with questions about the old Zenshodō and other matters concerning the neighborhood. So I kept quiet and took advantage of my privileges as a prospective buyer to pick out a few records and listen to them. When I was a boy I had once received a 24-hole harmonica as a prize for one of the funny stories I had submitted to *Young People's Club*. That had led me to sign up for a harmonica study group called The Lemonade Club when I entered middle school, and for a while I took an intense interest in music. I recalled those times as I listened to the records.

When I had finished, I found my throat was dry and asked the proprietor if I could have a glass of water. "Indeed you may!" he said and went off to fetch it. While he was gone I took out my wallet and checked to see how much money I had. When the proprietor returned with the glass of water, he carefully dusted off the counter before setting it down.

I bought a couple of records and was preparing to leave when it started raining. I guessed it was only a passing shower that would let up in a minute and settled back to wait for a little. But, far from showing signs of letting up, the rain began coming down in earnest. The proprietor noticed me looking at my watch and said that if I was in a hurry he would be happy to lend me an umbrella.

I accepted his offer, and was on my way home from the ward office and about to board a streetcar when my eyes happened to light on the Yano family seal on the umbrella the proprietor had lent me. Yano—of course! For the first time it came to me who he was.

In the Yoshida area of Kyōto, where students of the Third High School and Kyōto University lived, there had been a Western-style restaurant called Yano Seiyōken. It now came to me that the man who had run the restaurant was none other than the proprietor of the music store where I had borrowed the umbrella. Ten years or more had gone by, so it was no wonder I couldn't remember where I'd seen him, even though the face looked familiar. Once I had made the connection, however, I found I could recall quite a few things about him.

Ever since my student days I have been in the habit of going off eating and drinking or on shopping expeditions without making certain just how much money I have in my wallet, and as a result I have often found myself in great embarrassment when it came time to pay my bill. When this happened at Yano Seiyōken, the proprietor would generously allow me to put the amount on the tab, assuring me

I could pay it any time that was convenient. Pork sauté was the specialty of the house, but the other items on the menu were equally good, especially the vegetables in vinegar, and you could have all the celery you wanted for free. In addition, the owner kept stocked up on the latest records to play for his customers, all of them recordings of the type of Western music that students favored.

Recalling those days, I couldn't help wondering at what a coincidence it was that I had run into the same man again, and when I went to the record store some ten days later to return the umbrella, I reminded the proprietor of our earlier acquaintance.

"Well, well—so it was you. No wonder I thought I had seen you somewhere before," he said. "But I would hardly recognize you now." He added this not as a compliment but rather as a fact that had just come to his notice. And then, agreeing that it was a peculiar coincidence indeed, he filled me in on the events in his own life.

He had originally been a seaman, he told me. From the time he was a young boy he had been employed on ships engaged in the European run. He had worked as a stoker in the engine room or as a cook or dishwasher, and then at the age of forty had given up life at sea and opened a Western-style restaurant in the Yoshida area of Kyōto. But he had perhaps been a bit too confident in his skill as a cook. He forgot about business and thought only about how to get the best ingredients and serve the tastiest meals at the lowest prices to his student customers. It got to be a kind of hobby with him and he paid no attention to the earnings, so that the losses piled up month after month and in the end he was forced to close the place.

When he had finished getting rid of the equipment and

tying up all the loose ends, he was left with a huge stack of records, the records for which he had ungrudgingly paid out such sums of money each month so his student-customers would have something to listen to. These alone he couldn't bear to part with, so he brought them along when he moved here to Ōsaka, and they had inspired him to open his present music store. He went on to add that he had not gone to all the trouble of setting up business in this out-of-the-way neighborhood because of any hopes of brisk sales, but because the rent on the store and the living quarters that went with it was inexpensive. "When you start worrying about how much the rent is, I guess you've come to the end of the line as a businessman," he added in a burst of self-derision.

"I've run a restaurant and a record store and worn myself out doing all sorts of things that are no use to anyone. It was probably a mistake ever to have come ashore at the age of forty. I'm sorry now I put that thing up for a decoration," he exclaimed, pointing to the life preserver hanging on the wall. "Still, I'm only fifty-three . . ."

Just then a young boy entered the store, a school satchel on his back, and murmured a brief greeting to the proprietor, who was evidently his father.

"Here now, Shinbō—aren't you going to say hello to the gentleman?" his father asked, but the boy by this time had slipped out of sight in the rear of the store.

"Not much of a talker," the proprietor apologized, though with a look of delight. "He comes up for promotion to middle school soon and I'm worried how he'll do in his oral interview," he explained, suddenly lowering his voice. "Unlike his father, he doesn't have very much to say."

"If I remember, you had two children . . ."

"Oh yes, the older girl. When you knew her she was just about the boy's age. She finished girls' school a long time ago and now she works for a company in the Kitahama financial district." His voice returned to its normal pitch as he said this.

Just as I got ready to leave, it started to rain. "I seem to be some kind of rainmaker," I said with a smile of apology. As a result, I was obliged once more to borrow the umbrella that I had brought back. This meant I would have to come once more to return it; in other words, I would have another excuse to visit the neighborhood. Mulling over this coincidence, I thought of the even stranger quirk of fate represented by the music store, whose proprietor had earlier been in business in Yoshida in Kyōto, where I passed the second phase of my youth, and had now moved to this neighborhood, where I passed the first phase. As I descended Kuchinawa Slope in the rain, those two dim and far-away eras in my life came flooding back, their memories superimposed one on the other.

When I went to return the umbrella half a month or so later, the proprietor announced as soon as he saw me that his son Shinbō had failed to make it into middle school.

"Is the competition at that school really that stiff?" I exclaimed, and then by way of consolation added, "Well, never mind. He can try again next year."

But the proprietor merely remarked in an offhand manner that he had persuaded his son to abandon the thought of further study and to take a job as a newspaper delivery boy. When I expressed surprise, he explained that he had thought it important for his daughter to go through girls' school because if she didn't, she would be at a great disadvantage when it came time to get married. "In the case of a boy, though, even without a lot of schooling, if he knows how to do a day's work he can get along perfectly well in the world and be of use to others," he assured me. "So I got him to give up his studies, which he was never good at anyway, and to take this job delivering papers where he can learn how to work. If you start from childhood accustoming a person to the habit of physical labor, he'll turn out a better human being, I do believe!"

Going down the stone steps of Kuchinawa Slope in the hush of twilight, I ran into a young boy coming up the steps from the street below. He gave a quick nod of his head and as he brushed past me, a pile of newspapers under his arm, I saw that it was Shinbō, the son of the record store proprietor.

After that I saw him on a number of occasions, dragging his feet wearily as he returned to the store from his newspaper rounds. He was always silent as he slid open the glass-paneled door, and would disappear into the rear of the store without speaking even to his father. I would be there listening to records, and I wondered if he refrained from speaking on my account or whether it was just his natural reticence. His eyebrows were rather thin but his features were well-formed and attractive and his bare legs below the pair of short pants he wore were white as a girl's.

As soon as he came home from work, I would always ask the proprietor to shut off the phonograph. I did this so the proprietor would have a chance to talk to his son, as he often did, calling to him to go to the public bath or to help himself to the cookies that had come in the allotment of food rations. His remarks were usually answered by no more than a cursory grunt from the rear of the store. But I could sense the deep affection that existed between father and son, and it affected me more strongly than the music that I came to the store to hear.

When summer came I got busy with preparations for the Reservists' Association inspection and other matters connected with the reserve military forces, as well as with my own personal affairs, and for a while I had no opportunity to visit the record store. The first of July was the date for the annual festival at the nearby Aizendō temple in Yūhigaoka. The daughter of the record store proprietor had told me that on that day the daughters of Ōsaka families who had reached the age for such things would put on their summer kimonos and go to show them off to Aizen Myōō, the Buddhist deity who presides over affairs of the heart. But I was too busy to attend the festival.

July 9th was the summer festival at Ikutama Shrine, and by that time I had finished with the military exercises. I decided I would go to the festival—for the first time in ten years—and take the son of the record store proprietor along for company. I was looking forward to buying him a few little things at the night stalls that would no doubt be set up in the grounds of the shrine, and for that reason I deliberately waited until evening before going to the store to pick him up. When I arrived there, however, I was told he had recently been drafted as a civilian laborer and assigned to work in a factory in Nagoya, and that he was now living in the dormitory attached to the factory. On the way to the record store I had stopped at a drugstore and bought some Metabolin vitamin pills, thinking that the boy could use them. These I now handed over to the father, asking him to send them to Shinbō, and then, without thinking to stop and listen to a record, went off to the festival alone.

I once again got busy with my work and had no time to think about the music store, and so the summer went by. When insects came bumbling into my room, I batted at them with my fan, supposing that they were the rambunctious summer variety. But they would just make a faint melancholy chirring noise and drop to the floor, and I realized that autumn was already upon us. One day a postcard arrived from the music store informing me that a record I had been searching for was now available and I could pick it up any time I wished to stop by. Judging from the handwriting, the card had been written by the daughter.

The record in question was an old recording by Charles Panzera of Henri DuParc's setting of Baudelaire's "*L'invitation au voyage.*" I had had a copy of the record when I was living as a student in Kyōto, but a girl who used to come to my room from time to time accidentally broke it. Perhaps because she felt upset about what she had done, she never came to see me again. She was stockily built and terribly nearsighted. About two years ago I ran into her younger sister, who for some reason knew that we were acquainted, and she told me that the girl had died. The news brought back memories of days that could now never be relived. So this particular record had very special associations for me. I had been devoting myself to writing, an occupation that by rights ought inevitably to set one to mulling over one's youthful experiences. And yet I had gotten so busy in my work that for a time I had actually forgotten all about my own younger days. As I glanced at the postcard, however, memories of them all at once came welling up, and for the first time in several months I set off for Kuchinawa Slope.

When I got to the music store, I found that the proprietor was not there. His daughter was minding the store alone and reported that her father had gone to Nagoya the previous evening. Fortunately it was Sunday, her day off, so she had been able to take over the store for him.

When I inquired further, I found that Shinbō had come home from the factory the previous evening, though he had not been given permission to do so. It seems that the night before, he had been lying in the factory dormitory listening to the rain when all of a sudden he had a tremendous yearning to see his family. He wanted to be sleeping once more in the same room with his father and his sister. The longing had been like nothing he had ever known before—it had in fact been too strong for him—and the next day he had simply gotten on the train and come home.

This was the story he told, but his father would have none of it. He refused to let the boy stay even that one night but put him right on the night train and went with him to make sure he returned immediately to Nagoya. "I felt sorry for Shinbō—having to go back without even one night at home," the daughter observed, and there was something very adult in her tone, something quite in keeping with her twenty-five years.

Twenty-five—almost past the age for getting married, I thought. But in her clear, innocent gaze there was a look of untroubled youthfulness. The face I had remembered from our Kyōto days, when she had just entered girls' school, was still there, particularly around the cheeks, and I was struck by the frank way she revealed her affection and concern for her brother in the serious way she spoke of him.

As far as affection went, however, I guessed she was no match for the fifty-some-year-old father. She told me that before her father and brother had left for Nagoya, her father had gotten out the old kitchen knife he had used in his restaurant days and had done his best to fix a nice box of food for his son to eat on the train.

I was touched by the fatherly concern that I perceived in the gesture. But when I put in an appearance at the record store ten days later, the proprietor launched into a quite unexpectedly vehement condemnation of his son. The father had managed to talk Shinbō into going back to his job at the factory, I was told, but every few days a letter would come from him saying how much he missed his family. "If you go off to work somewhere, what good does it do to keep on wishing you were home!" the father exclaimed in exasperation. "From the time I was a boy until I was forty I lived aboard ship, but whatever corner of the world I happened to be in, I never once acted in that kind of crybaby fashion! A damned fool—that's what he is!" the proprietor shouted at me, as though I were to blame. I realized then that he could be much more severe on his son than I would have supposed.

It was dusk by the time I started home. As I passed the temples along the way, I caught the scent of fragrant olive drifting on the night air, coming from the bushes in bloom at this season.

Then it was winter. I heard that Shinbō had once more made his way home from Nagoya and once more had been scolded and sent back to the factory, and again I felt a pang of sympathy. But circumstances kept me away from the music store. Sometimes I wondered how the proprietor and his daughter were getting along, and whether Shinbō was hard at work at his job. And I also worried a little, thinking that the music store people might miss me because I had suddenly stopped coming after being such a frequent caller in the past. But I had gotten rather lazy about going out anywhere, and in fact my health was such that it was all I could do to keep on top of my work. So I neglected my duty to my friends, though I knew I ought to go see them—somehow Kuchinawa Slope seemed too far away. And as my memories of the record store slipped into the past, the year drew to a close.

But the year-end season always sets one to thinking of others, and when New Year's came and I wondered if I would ever see my music store friends again, I had a sudden urge to visit them, and in fact thought it would be very bad of me if I didn't. So, although I was still suffering from a cold, I made my way up Kuchinawa Slope. Halfway up I stopped to catch my breath and remove the gauze mask I was wearing over my nose and mouth.

When I arrived in front of the music store, I found the door tightly shut and a notice pasted on it: "Business discontinued due to the condition of the times." I rapped on the door, thinking there must be someone inside, but got no answer. When I looked, I saw the door had been locked from the outside.

"Have they moved away?" I inquired of the old man in the nameplate store next door.

"Gone to Nagoya."

"Nagoya—where the son is?"

"That's right," the old man nodded. "The boy missed his family. No matter what they said to him he kept wanting to come home. His father tried everything he could think of, but finally he moved the family to Nagoya. He figures if they can all live and work together, the boy won't feel lonely anymore. It was the only way to stop him from wanting to come home all the time. And anyway, the father was afraid if he stayed here much longer he might be drafted for some work assignment himself. So about three weeks ago he shut up the shop and went off with his daughter. She quit her job at the company—says she's going to work at the same factory as the boy.

"When it's for your own flesh and blood," the old man added, droning along in a low voice, "you'll do almost anything."

He must be over seventy, I thought as I watched him take off his glasses and wipe the rheum from his eyes. He apparently had not recognized me as someone who grew up in the neighborhood, and I decided I didn't want to remind him.

The trees along Kuchinawa Slope were bleak and bare, and a chill winter wind raced through them. As I descended the stone steps it occurred to me that I probably would not be going up and down them again for some time to come. The pleasant recollections of my youthful years had come to an end, it seemed, and some quite new reality had now swung around into position to confront me. The wind rattled sharply in the tops of the trees.

Translated by Burton Watson

The Swallows' Nest

Miyamoto Teru

YOSHITAKE KENJI, president of the Dream Street Shopping Arcade Merchants' Association, abruptly slid open the little glass window, pointed to the eaves, and said, "We want to get rid of this swallows' nest." Tomi opened her sunken eyes in surprise. How long did a swallow live? The question had preoccupied her recently, and just then she'd been absorbed in thoughts about swallows.

"Get rid of it?" Like Yoshitake, she spoke the language of southern Ōsaka.

"That's right. There was a meeting of the Association last night. A majority vote. People said the swallows' nest under the eaves of this tobacco stand impedes the future development of the Dream Street Shopping Arcade."

"Why is that?"

MIYAMOTO TERU (1947–) is a prolific author of short stories, essays, and novels. In 1977 he received the Dazai Osamu Prize for *Doro no kawa* (Muddy River), and in 1978 he received the Akutagawa Prize, the most coveted literary prize for young Japanese writers, for *Hotarugawa* (River of Fireflies). This selection is the second chapter of *Yumemidōri no hitobito* (The People of Dream Street), a series of stories about the lower-class workers in an Ōsaka shopping arcade.

Yoshitake cleared his throat, leaned forward, and glanced around the interior of Tomi's shop as he groped for words. "Well, you see, well . . ." In fact, it was not the swallows' nest he wanted to dislodge, but Tomi, who held the rights to a one-mat space in the Furukawa Stationery Shop. Trying to look both stern and gentle at the same time, he knitted his brows and smiled. The demands that this attempt made on his facial muscles gave rise to faint twitches all over. Rattled, he rubbed his face with both hands.

"We've got to make plans to attract customers from farther away. We've got to make the shops look more modern. People have been saying so for a long time, and that's why Mr. Tai repainted his walls and enlarged his showwindow. The Muratas remodeled their clock shop last summer, too. And it seems the Furukawas want to strip off this dirty old siding and replace it with a mortar wall. The swallows' nest will be in the way."

Tomi gave this some thought. "And the people of the shopping arcade decided by majority vote to get rid of the swallows' nest, so the Furukawas can renovate their shop?" She couldn't believe that the Dream Street crowd would exchange opinions about a swallows' nest for the benefit of someone else's shop. She knew everything about the people of Dream Street—their family customs, their financial problems, their secret thoughts. For thirty-four years, Iseki Tomi had been sitting in her three-by-six shop in a corner of the shopping arcade, watching the residents through her little glass window. She simply watched; she was no busybody, peering into people's houses. But she'd come to know the residents of the arcade as well as if she'd placed them, one by one, on the palm of her hand and studied them. For thirty-four years, since the age of forty-three, she'd looked out silently and guilelessly from her sunless shop; and, though she didn't realize it, she'd gained from this the power to see people.

Yoshitake was angry with himself for letting this oval-faced old woman, her white hair pulled back in a bun, give him a hard time; but he mustn't let her suspect that the Furukawas had asked him to get her out.

"As it is, you've got to feel sorry for the swallows," he said, changing strategy. "When they come back and find their nests gone, they'll probably be confused at first. But if they fly just a little way into the country, they'll find lots of places where the air is cleaner and there's more to eat than here in the dirty old city. They'll size up the situation, move to the country, and build new nests. I think they'd be happier there; don't you?"

"Yes, you may be right."

Hearing Tomi's response, Yoshitake Kenji thought his spontaneous change in strategy had worked. He'd better not steamroll ahead; it'd be smarter to give Tomi a little time. "The swallows'll be coming soon," he said, with a the-atrical glance at the sky. Then he headed back toward Dream Hall, the pachinko parlor he operated. Tomi glanced at the plywood partition separating her shop from the stationer. The Furukawas might be desperate to get rid of her, she thought, but she held an irrefutable certificate of title. Dark, damp, and enclosed on three sides with ply-wood, Tomi's tobacco stand resembled an isolation cell. Stacks of cardboard boxes, full of cigarettes, threatened to collapse on her if she didn't move carefully. It was the

Furukawas who'd turned Tomi's stand into an isolation cell. There'd been no plywood partition five years ago; but when the Furukawas decided to install a new display case and decorate the wall behind it with stylish wallpaper, they didn't negotiate—they issued something close to a peremptory demand, and Tomi could only acquiesce.

The Furukawa Stationery Shop originally belonged to Tomi's husband. Four years after the end of World War II the postwar black markets were either razed or turned into shopping districts. The name "Dream Street Shopping Arcade" was imposed on the place by people who began to use it as their base of operations long after Tomi had come. Before that, it'd been a tidied-up black market, a nameless shopping street on the edge of Ōsaka. Tomi's husband, who worked for a large stationer in Kitahama before the war, had considered his age, sold off the Kōchi farmland his parents had left him, and bought property which provided both a business and a residence on this shopping street. Having lost their only son on the battlefield, she and her husband nurtured no bold desires or dreams; it would be enough if they could maintain a business and a residence that would allow them to live quietly together. Less than six months after opening the shop, Tomi's husband died. On his way home from the bath one evening, he'd suddenly pressed a hand to his chest, dropped to his knees, and expired right there on the street. Tomi knew nothing about running a business. In that time of shortages, it was nearly impossible for a woman on her own to stock notebooks and pencils. Just as she was wondering what to do, Furukawa Ken'ichi, who'd worked with her husband in Kitahama before the war, came calling and offered to buy the land and the shop. Tomi was within an ace of accepting his proposal without question, but then a little incident taught her some worldly wisdom. Ten days after her husband's sudden death, she bought a skinny daikon which turned out to be rotten inside when she sliced it with a kitchen knife. She took it back to the greengrocer the next day to complain. In twenty-four hours, the price of daikon had doubled. She asked for a new daikon in exchange for the spoiled one. The greengrocer replied that Tomi had chosen the vegetable herself and it was too late to make an exchange. Tomi was too timid to argue.

"It's inflation, ma'am, inflation," said the grocer. "See for yourself. The very same daikon costs twice as much today. Things the way they are nowadays, you don't know what'll happen to your money. It's like waste paper. *Things* are worth more than scraps of paper. Throw away the spoiled part, cut the outside into strips, and boil it with soy sauce. That's better than buying a new daikon at these prices, isn't it?"

Tomi started for home, clutching the daikon to her breast. So there's no telling how far paper money will fall in value, she said to herself. She mustn't be in a rush to sell her property to Furukawa Ken'ichi. She pictured herself staring blankly at a bundle of worthless yen notes. When Furukawa came calling the next day, Tomi told him she'd decided not to sell. Furukawa persisted. When Tomi haltingly explained her reasons, Furukawa offered a compromise. He really wanted to acquire the entire property, but he'd be willing to leave Tomi with a piece of her own. That way she'd retain the space to carry on a small business, enough to support herself as a woman living alone, and she'd also secure the money she needed right away. Pondering this, Tomi decided it was indeed a splendid plan; but she asked Furukawa to wait several days for her reply. In that short time, she'd consider what sort of business she could handle. She consulted her only relative, her late husband's younger brother.

"No physical work, no complicated purchasing or transactions, and a small space—that would be a tobacco stand." Such was her brother-in-law's conclusion. A tobacco stand. What a good idea. It would be a cash business; and since tobacco was now a state monopoly, she'd heard, she'd never be cheated on her purchases; all she'd have to do was to sit in her shop. She could handle that. The net profit would be small, of course, but she needed just enough to live alone modestly. Tomi made up her mind.

Furukawa looked relieved. "Two mats of space would be enough for a tobacco stand, wouldn't it? Wait, you won't need two mats, you can do a fine business with just one!" His manner betrayed his eagerness to get the name on the registration changed to his own as quickly as possible. Asking her brother-in-law to serve as a witness, Tomi handed the registration papers to Furukawa in exchange for the money. Then she checked, again and again, the certificate granting her the right to use one mat's space of the land and the building, facing the street on the east side of the stationery shop; and she had Furukawa press his seal to it.

Less than four days after Tomi had hung out the sign of her tobacco stand, a pair of swallows began to build a nest under the projecting eaves of her tile roof. Watching the two swallows laboring on their nest with what seemed to her both heroism and desperation, Tomi murmured to herself, "Swallows are building a nest under the roof of my shop."

She began to feel confident that good fortune in some form, however slight, would visit her life from now on. This was not just because of the saying that happiness comes to a house where swallows build their nests. Recalling how the swallows had flitted back and forth under the eaves of her shop for two days before they began their work, Tomi decided that the swallow couple, having decided to nest here, had mutely been seeking her permission and, at the same time, had been observing what kind of person she was. In her loneliness, Tomi felt as though she were being blessed unexpectedly with children. She knew nothing about swallows, except that they flew in from the south in the spring, laid their eggs, hatched and raised their chicks, and returned to the south in the fall. She didn't really know which countries in "the south," but she fantasized that her son, drafted by the army and killed in battle on New Guinea, had come back to his mother in the form of a swallow. No good came of being born a human. How much more fortunate to be reborn as a swallow and soar freely in the sky. A swallow wouldn't be forced to join the army, leave his loved ones, and carry a rifle when he had no desire to kill anyone. With these thoughts in her heart, Tomi would step from her shop many times during the day to watch as the earthen, bowl-shaped nest grew. She welcomed these unexpected dependents. She even felt love for the agile birds, wrapped in their greenish-black luster. When the rain continued to fall for days on end, concern that the chicks would starve caused her to lose her appetite. In the years that followed, Tomi learned several things about swallows. They usually laid four to six eggs. It was almost always the female that sat on the eggs, and the eggs would hatch in about three weeks. The swallows didn't necessarily return to the same nest every year.

In the years when April passed without the swallows returning to their nest under the tile roof of her shop, Tomi would feel alone in the world, and her thoughts would turn to the past. In years when the swallows came, relief and joy would turn her thoughts to the future. She believed that only death lay in her future. But when the swallows returned and laid their eggs, and Tomi finally heard the robust squawking of the chicks demanding food, it seemed to her that death was the beginning of something new. She would be imbued with a strange, quiet courage.

She always kept the shop open until eight o'clock at night. At seven-thirty, she'd put the day's proceeds into a small leather pouch with a long string attached and tie it firmly around her waist. Locking the glass window, she'd step into the narrow alley that separated her from the neighboring White Lily Beauty Parlor, lock the door of her shop, and return to her apartment, a ten-minute walk from the Dream Street Shopping Arcade.

As Tomi got ready to go home that night, she wondered why Yoshitake Kenji, who undoubtedly had been solicited by the Furukawas, began his scheme to oust her by trying to get rid of the swallows' nest. Even if the nest vanished, there'd be no incentive for her to move out. The day her tobacco stand disappeared from a corner of the Furukawa Stationery Shop would be the day she died. There was no need to hurry things along. With a hand over her heart, which had begun to beat irregularly these two or three years, she opened the glass window and leaned out. She looked toward the entrance of the shopping arcade. For a time she waited for Satomi Shunta to come home from work, but finally she gave up. She liked the young Satomi Shunta. It's true there was something muddleheaded in his expression and in the way he spoke; but there were also times when a single-minded passion, obstinacy, and resolve would flash in his eyes like the gleam of a dog's eyes in the dark. Her son, killed in battle at the age of twenty, had had the same quality. Tomi would think of her beloved son whenever she spoke with Satomi Shunta, and for an instant a fierce anger would raise gooseflesh on her frail body. Her anger was directed neither at the enemy nation nor at the soldier who'd killed him, but at the Japanese policy makers who, with a simple postcard, would snatch a son from his mother, a husband from his wife. Like most old people, Tomi lived in the past more often than not. Sometimes she'd gaze into the distance with unfocused eyes and drift into a reverie as she recalled the day she first took her five-year-old son to the beach, or the way he trotted back and forth naked between the men's and women's sections of the public bath, even after he'd reached the fifth grade. It was always at such times that Satomi Shunta came to buy cigarettes. A coincidence, no doubt; but it was also a reason for the special feelings that Tomi had for Shunta.

Tomi locked the door of her shop and took five or six steps before she heard the roar of motorcycles. Two bikes came streaking down the middle of Dream Street and slammed on their brakes near Tomi. Two helmeted men clutching long, steel bars jumped off the bikes and smashed the glass window of Tomi's shop. Then they broke through the wood siding, sent the sign flying, snapped the lock, stepped into the shop, and tossed all the unopened cardboard boxes out onto the pavement. Using the pointed ends of their steel bars, they made a honeycomb of the walls, and then began to punch holes in the cartons of new cigarettes. Tomi at first had no idea what was going on.

"That should do it," said one of the men. As the motorcycles disappeared, the residents of the shopping arcade came running. Tomi knew: it wasn't that the bikes were gone by the time the residents arrived; the residents watched the bikes go before they flocked to the scene.

"What happened?" It was the voice of the son and heir to the Tai Liquor Store.

"Tomi-san, are you all right?" This was the voice of Mr. Wang, of the Tarōken Chinese restaurant.

Dizzy, Tomi staggered. She felt sick at her stomach. Her heart raced, then stopped, then began to beat wildly again. She sat heavily on the pavement. She thought that she was still standing. She moved her legs, intending to walk toward the shop; but what the residents saw was Tomi falling slowly backward, to all appearances dead.

The police had to wait three days before they could take Tomi's statement. She regained consciousness as soon as the ambulance brought her to the hospital; but her arrhythmia showed no improvement, and she began talking to herself. Her words, now mingled with tears, now with smiles, grew more passionate with time and flowed ceaselessly from her mouth.

"If you wave your net around like that, you'll break the dragonflies' wings. Foolish boy, only catching drone beetles. I'll have to get your father to scold you. Ah! Watch where you're going. How many times do I have to tell you? Watch where you're going when you walk in the street, or you'll fall in the sewage ditch. The next time you fall in the ditch, I won't let you off with just a knock on the forehead. What's this? You come back crying from a fight with a girl? And then you hit Mother's behind. You couldn't win an argument with a girl, could you? Crybaby. Aha, you're hiding something from Mother. You can't fool me. You came from inside me, you know. . . ."

The doctor injected a strong sedative and set up a continuous intravenous drip of nutrients mixed with a cardiac. Then he spoke to Satomi Shunta, who'd arrived out of breath at the hospital twenty minutes after Tomi was carried in, and had been at her side ever since: the shock had left her in a temporary state of dementia. The electrocardiogram showed indications of severe angina pectoris; he intended to carry out a detailed examination when her condition stabilized. . . .

Gazing at the ceiling, Tomi continued her soliloquy after the doctor left the room. "People go on about unfilial children, and a child who dies before his parents is the most unfilial of all. But you're not unfilial. You were dragged off by the army and killed in the war. You were twenty. Did you have a girlfriend? It's all right, Mother's here."

Tomi's voice grew fainter, then intermittent, until finally she closed her eyes. Fearfully, Satomi Shunta held the palm of his hand to her nostrils. She was breathing. Relieved, he left the room, went to the smoking area, and lit a cigarette. He felt an uncontrollable anger toward something he couldn't define. It wasn't directed at the two men who destroyed Tomi's shop, nor at the people of Dream Street who looked on from their shop fronts and second-floor windows without intervening. He didn't sleep that night, sitting in a chair beside Tomi's bed. He mulled over the words she'd been mumbling to herself. It was after three o'clock in the morning when Tomi's pulse returned to normal and the thick intravenous needle was pulled from a blood vessel in her arm. And it was then that Shunta finally realized that the loathing he felt was for all of society, or, in other words, for humanity itself. Tomi had never told Shunta anything about her past. Nevertheless, he felt as though he understood completely, from Tomi's demented, disjointed, but not incoherent mumblings, what this woman's seventy-seven years of life had been.

With the doctor's permission, a middle-aged policeman asked Tomi if she had any idea who was responsible. Confidently, her voice shaking slightly, she replied, "I think it was Yoshitake Kenji and Mr. and Mrs. Furukawa." Anger brought tears to her small, sunken eyes. Tomi explained how for decades the Furukawas had wanted to evict her, how they'd harassed her in countless ways to that end, and how Yoshitake—on the very day of the incident—had come to threaten her over the swallows' nest. There was no doubt in Tomi's mind. As evidence, she told the policeman, "Two days before, the Furukawas said there was a death in the family and went to Nagoya. They closed the shop and went away to hide the fact that they were behind it all. There's no question about it."

She'd lived honestly; she'd never done anything to cause anyone resentment. After making this assertion, Tomi began to have difficulty breathing and pressed a hand to her chest. The doctor was called; the electrocardiogram machine was brought in. The paroxysm passed quickly.

Yoshitake was summoned to the police station first. Word spread in a flash among the residents of Dream Street Shopping Arcade.

"It's just the sort of thing Yoshitake might do," said Wang of the Tarōken to the butcher-shop brothers, as they wolfed down pot-stickers and gulped their beer. The brothers knew they'd been nicknamed the "Ox Twins," but they didn't know that the people of the arcade gossiped about them constantly and even distinguished between them by calling the older one the Black Ox and the younger one the Red Ox. In fact the brothers weren't twins; three years separated them. Still, in facial appearance and stature they looked enough alike to be twins. Tatsumi Ryūichi, the older one, had a dusky complexion. Ryūji, his younger brother, earned his nickname from the way his face, neck, and chest turned crimson when he was excited. They shared a wild temperament and a tendency to fight when they drank; the elder, in particular, had until three years before been a member of the yakuza organization that dominated southern Ōsaka. He wore long-sleeved shirts, even in summer, to cover the tattoos that spread from his back to his elbows. He'd reformed and, following in his father's footsteps, ran the butcher shop harmoniously with his younger brother; but no one knew when his true nature might reassert itself. Everyone on Dream Street believed this, but no one would say it. They were afraid of what might happen if they let something slip and the brothers got wind of it.

"Yeah, but what good does it do Yoshitake to trash the old lady's shop? She already had one foot in the grave," Ryūichi said to Wang, a toothpick in his mouth.

"It's Furukawa. Furukawa. Listen. Yoshitake wants to run for the ward assembly next year. He needs money. He's gotta round up votes, too. And Old Man Furukawa can deliver six hundred votes."

"Six hundred votes? How can Old Man Furukawa do that?" When Ryūji was angry his face grew red, but when he drank it went pale. Now his face showed considerable interest. Wang sat down before the Ox Twins and spoke as if he were revealing a momentous secret.

"You know that weird religion called the Light of Happiness?"

The Ox Twins glanced at Wang skeptically. "Don't know it," they replied.

"The founder's a woman. They say light shines from her fingertips. If that light touches you, it cures all your diseases, and your business prospers. With that line they've recruited some three thousand members in the last ten years. The headquarters are about ten minutes west of here by car, and so most of the believers are concentrated around this area. I've heard there are six hundred just in this ward!"

Wang paused for a moment, then lowered his voice. "Furukawa is the founder's little brother. In the last election for the prefectural assembly, Furukawa took some money from the conservative incumbent and collected votes from the Light of Happiness. Six hundred votes don't count for much in a prefectural election, but at the ward level, it's enough to make a candidate drool. If Furukawa asked him to get rid of the old lady, Yoshitake couldn't refuse."

"So that's it," The Black Ox laughed, and the Red Ox clapped Wang on the shoulder. "You're pretty smart!"

Pleased with himself, Wang poured beer for the brothers. "You'll see. Pretty soon the police'll be after Furukawa!"

Wang was startled to see the brothers exchange glances and smile. Maybe the two men with their faces hidden under helmets had been the Ox Twins. The blood drained from Wang's face. He couldn't sleep a wink that night. He'd blabbed the whole plot to the butcher brothers, and they were tools of Yoshitake and Furukawa. He'd be next. Wang pictured himself being stuffed into the trunk of the Ox Twin's car, carried off into the mountains, and buried alive, still bound hand and foot. He shook his wife awake. "I might be killed," he mumbled, his eyes bleary.

His wife pulled him down by the collar of his pajamas, covered him with a quilt, and said, "You're having a silly dream. Go to sleep or you'll be late for school tomorrow." Half asleep, she took her husband for her daughter.

Wang's anxiety and fear were immediately resolved, however. Someone had seen license numbers the night of the incident and reported them by telephone to the police, who immediately turned up the names of two high-school students. The boys played dumb at first, but confessed when the policemen told them, "The longer it takes you to come clean, the longer you'll be in the reformatory!" The crime arose from a trivial incident. The Furukawas had five sons. The youngest, a high-school student, failed his university entrance exams. Drinking some sake to dull the disappointment, he went to a nearby park, where he sat on a bench in the cold wind, despairing of the world. With an ear-splitting roar, two boys in helmets and leather jackets rode up on motorcycles and began to race around the park. The Furukawa boy was furious. Emboldened by sake, he picked up a piece of wood and threw it toward the bikes. It struck the boy riding in front, right on the head. The boy and his bike toppled over, and the second bike, following close behind, struck the first and went flying. The Furukawa boy ran away in a panic, but then began to worry and looked back. The two riders had been watching their assailant run away, even as they lay writhing on the ground; and now they had a clear view of his face, since he'd stopped under a street light. As it happens, the two bikers were students at the same high school as the Furukawa boy. One of them had broken a wrist, the other a leg. During their recovery, they waited eagerly for the chance to have their revenge. The broken bones took nearly two months to mend. Then, that night, they mounted their bikes and barreled into the Dream Street Shopping Arcade, intending to smash the show window of the Furukawa Stationery Shop and break the youngest son's arm or leg. The shop always stayed open until ten o'clock, but for some reason the shutter was down and the second-floor lights were off, though it was still only eight. There was nothing to do but attack the tobacco stand. Since it occupied space in the same building, they assumed that Tomi's business was run by the Furukawa Stationery Shop.

When the police officer relayed these facts to her as she lay in bed, Tomi made a grim smile and weakly shook her head. "The police have been fooled. It was Furukawa and Yoshitake who wrecked my shop. There's no doubt about it."

The officer explained the matter in the minutest detail, but Tomi was not to be persuaded. Exasperated, he vented his anger to Yoshitake Kenji and the Furukawas: "The old lady'll hold a grudge against you until the day she dies. That's what you get for treating her badly all these years, just to gain one mat of shop space." He asked if there was anyone in the neighborhood whom Tomi trusted. Yoshitake and the Furukawas scratched their heads. Suddenly the officer remembered the young man who'd stayed beside Tomi the night she was taken to the hospital. "Oh. That was Mr. Satomi," said Mrs. Furukawa. She pointed to the second floor of the Wakana Fishcake Shop, diagonally across the street. Fixing his gaze on the fluorescent light shining from the second-floor window, the officer left a brusque parting shot: "I've done all I can. If you want to clear up the old lady's suspicions, the three of you should go ask for Satomi's help. Get him to convince her that you weren't the instigators. You bear some responsibility in this, Mr. and Mrs. Furukawa. It was your son who started it all. I'll be keeping an eye on you to see that you don't bully that lonely old lady any more."

The officer didn't sympathize with Tomi, nor was he driven by righteous indignation. He had no prospects for advancement in the seven years remaining before his retirement. The only pleasure left him was to pretend to side with the weak and browbeat anyone who had reason to feel guilty. His last words struck home. Yoshitake Kenji and the Furukawas made a beeline for the Wakana Fishcake Shop.

After returning from work the next day, Satomi Shunta bought a box of strawberries and headed for the hospital. Buying some milk at the hospital shop, he prepared the strawberries for Tomi as he did what Yoshitake and the

Furukawas had asked him to do—he tried to persuade Tomi with an exhaustive explanation. He saw right away that his efforts were wasted. Wrapped in a terrible despair by the unexpected disaster, and nearly drained of what little life force had been left, the old woman's mind hadn't returned to normal.

"They say the perpetrators' parents will pay for the repairs to your shop."

Tomi's face remained stiff, no matter what Shunta said. He was wondering why, when she suddenly spoke. "I suppose the swallows' nest was smashed, too."

"No, it's all right. It's still there under the eaves."

Shunta had forgotten to look into the life expectancy of sparrows, as Tomi had asked. "The encyclopedia only lists the varieties of swallows that come to Japan, shows their distribution with a map, and says that they return to North America and the Eurasian continent." At the bookstore he'd found several monographs on swallows, but none of them said how long a sparrow lives. He'd intended to go to the library and make a thorough study of the question, but he had forgotten about it after Tomi's incident.

"Where's the Furashan continent?"

"It's Eurasia, not Furashan."

"Eu . . . ra . . . sia." Bashfully, Tomi took out her false teeth. She said a strawberry seed between her teeth and gums was hurting her.

"The Eurasian continent is the region that includes Europe and Asia."

"Europe and Asia. Then, is New Guinea part of it?"

Shunta pictured the map of the world. He suspected

that New Guinea wasn't counted among the nations of Asia, but maybe strictly speaking, it was Asian territory.

"My son died in New Guinea."

Shunta was silent. He sensed that Tomi would begin talking again like one possessed, and he intended to listen. She seemed to be lost in thought, however, and said nothing more. Shunta picked up her false teeth, which were peeking out from under her pillow, took them to the bathroom, and washed them for her. He'd never realized that a little strawberry seed would be painful to an old person who wore dentures. Tomi's eyes were closed when he returned to her room. Seeing a tear make its way from the corner of her eye to her temple, Shunta was about to say something; but it occurred to him that she was probably thinking about her late son, and so he returned the dentures to her pillow, slipped from the room, and returned to his own roost.

Tomi wasn't thinking about her son. Surprised that Satomi Shunta would wash her dentures for her, Tomi felt her heart fill with gratitude. Those dirty things, she thought. Even a relative wouldn't want to touch them. . . . She wakened again and again during the night. Her hatred for Yoshitake Kenji and the Furukawas had continued to grow, but now it was crowded out by her gratitude to the youthful Shunta. Looking through the window of her room she knew that dawn was near. She knew that death, too, was near. Struggling to sit up, she began to write slowly with a ballpoint pen on a little memo pad. Finishing with the date and her name, she stamped the slip of paper with the water-buffalo-horn seal that she always carried with

her. She was out of breath; her heart made sounds like
bursting bubbles. Using the wrapping paper that had come
with Shunta's strawberries, she wrapped up the memo.
Then she groped for the plastic supper dish she'd left on
the table beside her bed. Her finger touched some hard
grains of rice. Using these instead of paste, she sealed each
and every opening in the fruitery paper that wrapped her
memo. Still not satisfied, she folded down the corners,
pasted them, then folded the papers double and pasted
them again. Her fingers shook; her vision grew dim. She'd
written that the rights to her tobacco stand and the
¥1,154,000 she'd diligently accumulated in a postal savings
account would go to Satomi Shunta upon her death.

Tomi asked herself whether her life had been fortunate
or unfortunate. She thought she'd probably been unfortunate. But now, at the very end, if she was not fortunate to
be able to leave everything to Satomi Shunta, who'd
allowed her to feel this deep gratitude, then what was good
fortune? Satomi Shunta, who somehow looked like her
son. This is what she said to herself as consciousness faded
away. The happiness that came to her on her deathbed
cancelled out the many misfortunes that had showered on
her until then. Tomi lived for another three hours, but she
never regained consciousness. She stopped breathing just
after seven o'clock in the morning.

Since Tomi had no close relatives, Yoshitake Kenji had
to see to every detail of her funeral, because he served as
Chairman of the Municipal Self-Governing Council in
addition to being President of the Dream Street Shopping
Arcade Merchants' Association. Yoshitake was furious
with himself for his stupidity in joining Furukawa's cam-

paign to oust Tomi. Summoned by the police, treated like a criminal, ridiculed by the residents of Dream Street Shopping Arcade—the very thought made him boil with rage, and there was no end in sight. On top of that, he had to track down an heir for the money Tomi left behind. He took out his anger on his wife and on the employees at his pachinko parlor. At the wake, he said to the directors of the Self-Governing Council, "I finally found one. Tomi's only relative."

"You found one, did you?" replied Tai Kikujirō.

"Her husband had a younger brother. But he died fifteen years ago. The brother had a daughter."

"You don't say."

"Well, I thought that was it. But two years after she gave birth, the daughter divorced her husband, and then in no time she died, too."

"You don't say."

"Then it really got difficult." Yoshitake emphasized the good faith and personal expense he'd expended in his search for Tomi's only living relative. "Tomi's brother-in-law's granddaughter is in Hokkaidō."

He spread out Tomi's possessions before the directors. A photograph of her husband; a photograph of her son, killed in the war; clothing; various small articles. The passbook for her postal savings account, and her seal. It was decided to put everything but the passbook and seal into the coffin with her. Yoshitake began to do so, with the directors as witnesses.

Tai Kikujirō held out an oddly shaped piece of folded paper on his palm. "What's this?" he said.

"That was beside Tomi's pillow," explained Yoshitake.

"Something seems to be wrapped inside. Shouldn't we open it?"

Yoshitake replied dismissively to the elderly Tai's comment. "It's nothing but origami. She probably made it to amuse herself at the hospital."

During the dispute over whether or not to open the little piece of wrapping paper, Satomi Shunta arrived to offer incense. After watching the director's exchange for a while, Shunta said diffidently, "It might be something she wouldn't want others to see. If you're going to open it, wouldn't it be best to ask the police to serve as witness?"

"It . . . it's nothing at all," said Yoshitake in confusion, as soon as he heard the word "police." "Let's . . . let's put it in the coffin. Right? Right? This wrapping paper is from the fruitery. She wouldn't wrap something important in this kind of paper."

"You're all sour on the police, now, aren't you," teased one of the directors. Blushing, Yoshitake placed Tomi's will, written with the last drop of her strength, in the coffin. And so the ¥952,000 that remained in Tomi's estate, after her funeral expenses had been deducted, went to Tomi's brother-in-law's granddaughter.

Translated by Anthony Hood Chambers

The Garden That Spirited My Dog Away

Tada Chimako

MIKI DIED. The dog we cared for over the course of sixteen years is dead. That is all, yet that is not all. Her death was not a normal one. For us, her owners, her death brought not only sadness but a sense of doubt that lingers like an unsolved mystery.

She was a Shiba-Inu, and although Shibas are relatively small dogs, she was on the small side even for her breed. The name Miki wasn't one we chose. Her pedigree papers

---

Before her death from cancer, TADA CHIMAKO (1930–2003) was known in Japan for her sensitive, erudite, and often surreal poetry, which often described the experiences of women in both the modern and ancient worlds. She published over a dozen volumes of poetry, several volumes of essays, and numerous distinguished Japanese-language translations of Marguerite Yourcenar, Saint-John Perse, and other French writers. The essay translated here describes the garden around Tada's own home, which sits on a sharply sloping street at the base of Mount Rokkō, the mountain that overlooks the city of Kōbe. It first appeared on the anniversary of her dog's death in September 2001.

came with the inscription "Princess Miki," and since it was almost too much trouble to think of another name, we went ahead and called her that. But our negligence did not end there. When we became busy, we cut corners and let her loose in the garden instead of walking her twice a day. When I think about it now, I realize how remiss we were as owners, just letting her out to exercise on her own. We were simply too wrapped up in ourselves to be troubled.

Whenever we went on an overnight trip, we'd always take her along. Before her, we had a mutt named Gorō, who with his Shepherd-like face was neat and handsome. Although he had a rather rough nature, he was also very nervous and got terribly carsick, which made it impossible to take him anywhere in the car. The car, however, never made Miki sick, and so we often took her places with us. She was such a complete contrast to Gorō that we were often amazed at what a big difference a dog's disposition could make. For instance, whenever Gorō had to go visit the veterinarian for a shot or something, just the mere scent of the doctor's white uniform or disinfectant would send him into a nervous frenzy. With bloodshot eyes, he'd try to make a run for it. If I didn't have a firm grip on his two front legs, he'd struggle for all he was worth. Miki, however, was as quiet and gentle as a lamb. Shots didn't seem to hurt her a bit.

About a decade or so ago, we decided to go to the hot springs in Okutsu. We also had something to do in the city of Okayama, and so we didn't go straight to our destination but instead stopped for a night in an Okayama hotel. Dogs weren't allowed inside so I suggested we put her to bed for the night in the corner of some storage shed, but that didn't go over too well. There was a plot of grass out back where people could park so I made the cold-hearted proposal that we tie her out there. My daughter Maya took offense at this. It looked like rain outside. If it rained during the night, wouldn't Miki get wet? So Maya came up with a plan.

A few years before, I had purchased a large, hand-woven palm-frond basket from an old lady in rural Egypt. For the trip I had filled it with towels and extra clothes. Maya decided we should take out the contents, put Miki inside, cover her with a bath towel, and sneak her into our room. The plan was that while I was completing the check-in procedures, Maya and my husband would carry the basket through the lobby and get in the elevator. When one of the porters noticed they were carrying something large, he flew to their side, stuck out his hand, and offered to carry it. Maya and my husband brushed him aside, telling him the basket was light. They'd carry it, no problem. When I saw them get onto the elevator alone, I followed.

It worked! We looked at one another and smiled in satisfaction. It never would have worked with Gorō, but Miki was calmer and had been as quiet as a mouse inside the basket. Still, once in the room, she paced nervously around the bed. Because she lived in the garden, she wasn't used to the indoors. Before bed that night, we set her on top of the toilet to do her business, but as she sat there on top of that smooth, artificial surface, it became clear that what ought to come out wouldn't. We were stuck. We decided we had to take her outside to the grass where the cars were parked. Of course, the plan was to bring her back inside as soon as she got finished.

There was an emergency staircase at the back of the hotel and because it was dark, Maya and I took her out by that route. The yard was pretty big, probably about four thousand square yards. After letting Miki get a bit of exercise, we saw that we had accomplished our goal, and I went to scoop her up. My daughter had gone ahead to the bottom of the stairs to see if the coast was clear. When she gave me the OK sign, I ran across the grass with Miki in my arms, but it was so dark I failed to notice a hole in the ground about five inches deep. As I rushed across, my right foot landed in it and slid wildly, pulling me down. When I fell, I twisted my ankle. A bolt of sharp pain shot up my leg. I dropped Miki and got into a kneeling position. Maya came running to me, asking me if I had tripped. With these words still hanging in the air, she scooped up Miki and dashed back up the stairway to our room.

Was my ankle sprained? I was in great pain. Dragging my lame leg behind me, I gradually made my way to the building and returned to the room—this time using the elevator, of course. My right ankle was swollen up like a balloon. I cooled it down in the bathroom under cold running water, but that didn't do any good. I couldn't make it to Okutsu. The next morning, I had them drop me at the bullet train stop in Okayama Station. I went home to Kōbe and went straight to the doctor. My husband, daughter, and Miki continued to Okutsu. I felt terribly cheated.

At the hospital, I was told I had broken some tiny bone on the outside of my foot, and they stuck me in a huge, overblown plaster cast that went almost all the way up to my knee. For an entire month, I had to rely on crutches to get around. Every time someone asked me what had happened to my foot, I would give them a full account of "Operation Smuggle Miki" at the hotel in Okayama.

The life of a dog is short. From a human point of view, even a dog that lives out the full span of its natural life dies terribly young. When we walked Miki in the hills behind our house, she crawled happily under bushes and ran up the sloping hills, rushing about at a pace several times faster than ours; but before we knew it, she overtook us on the slope of old age and passed us as we wandered along our paths to our final resting places. Still, as I said at the beginning, her death was not a normal one; but before I explain what happened to her, I should briefly describe the layout of the land around our house.

Our house sits on a sharply upward-sloping road at the base of Mt. Rokkō, the high mountain that overlooks the city of Kōbe. On the west side of our yard there is a small river flowing through a ravine. Our house is built on a flat plot of land, and at the back of the west side there is a stone staircase that leads downward toward the river. As you descend it stops at another hidden, narrow strip of yard that looks out over the river far below. Although we call this our hidden garden, we never tried to hide it from view. You simply cannot see into it because it is about thirteen feet lower than the upper portion of the yard. What's more, it is filled with trees that naturally hide it from view. West of this lower, hidden portion of the yard, there is a sharp drop to the shallow river, which flows through a ravine thirty-some feet below.

Because of the lay of the land, no fence is needed along the west side of our property. The sharp drop to the river forms a natural barrier that not even the most intrepid dog could possibly descend. The east side of our property runs along the sloping road in front of our house. Along it we have a stone wall high enough that a dog cannot jump over. We don't keep our dogs leashed. There have been times when we have opened the gate and they have slipped out past us, but Miki didn't have a tendency to wander. She would always come back and pace in front of the gate. Humans will ring bells to let people know they are there, but Miki would bark to let us know she had come home. Our street is on a sharp slope so the fences around the houses to the north and south of us are at quite different levels, but the granite-block walls are high enough that a dog cannot get over them. That's why we felt so comfortable letting Miki loose in the yard. To make matters worse, she had become hard of hearing, and her back legs were unsteady. A sixteen-year-old dog is, from the point of view of a human, equivalent to an octogenarian.

In one corner of the hidden portion of the yard was a pile of garden waste, mostly tree branches. (Gardening services charge a lot to haul away cut or fallen branches, so we just put them in a pile. This way, we saved what must have been hundreds of thousands of yen.) We had just left it there to compost, but one time Miki, whose legs were already weak, stepped into the pile, got caught, and couldn't break free. Oblivious to her predicament we went outside in the morning with her bowl of food and called her name. She didn't appear. As we started looking for her in the yard, we heard a pathetic whimper. Making our way to the brush pile, we saw our poor elderly dog wriggling among the withered

branches, caught in their trap. The heavy branches and little branches were all tangled together making it quite hard
to get her out. When we finally got her free she seemed
utterly exhausted, and for a little while, she didn't even have
the strength to drink the milk we gave her.

This experience taught me and my elderly husband that
we needed to build a barricade at the top of the staircase so
that she wouldn't go down into the hidden portion of the
yard above the river. We carried up several large branches
from the brush pile that had caught Miki, and we stuck
them into the thick azalea bushes on either side of the
stairway. In this way we created a low fence that our weak
dog couldn't possibly cross. This meant Miki could only run
around the flat, upper portion of the yard by our house.

Dogs have a natural tendency to walk around at night,
but because of her advanced age, Miki was even worse, like
a senile old lady wandering round and round the yard. As
she prowled around in the middle of the night, she would
sometimes start barking as if something were wrong. No
doubt her noise bothered our neighbors. At first we would
go look out every time, thinking that perhaps she had seen
a badger or wild boar. It is true that our neighborhood
serves as a virtual thoroughfare for boars descending Mt.
Rokkō to forage for food in the city. Still, there was never
any rhyme or reason to Miki's barking.

After about two weeks of this, my daughter, who had by
this time married and moved to Ashiya, came home for an
overnight stay. When she went out to give Miki her supper, she squatted in front of the doghouse, which we had
labeled with the sign MIKI'S HOUSE. As she hugged and

petted Miki, Maya talked to her—*Now Miki, you're a good girl. You shouldn't bark at night. You're bugging the neighbors. Sleep quietly, okay?*

That night was unusually quiet. We woke up the next morning in a good mood, commenting to each other that Miki must have listened to Maya's admonitions, but when it came time for Miki's breakfast, we realized she was gone. All three of us went out to look for her: Maya, my elderly husband, and I. We looked around the garden. At first it occurred to us that she might have broken through the barricade, descended into the lower portion of the yard, and gotten stuck again, but no, she was nowhere to be seen down there. Not knowing where else to look we went inside, commenting to each other that the gods seemed to have spirited her away. With dreary, worried looks on our faces, we sipped at our morning tea, which by this time had grown completely cold.

A few moments later, Maya got up, saying she was going to check the river. I followed. You cannot get to the river from our yard, but if you make a detour of a little more than two hundred yards there is a stone staircase by the gate of our neighbor to the south. From there you can descend to the river. Just as the houses around us are built on different levels along the sloping base of the mountain, the river flows down the base of the mountain along an incline, but just behind our house there is a place where the water flows over a man-made concrete structure and forms a tall waterfall. Below that, there is a pool of water where the water churns slowly. When you look at the river from our house, this spot falls right in a blind spot—or at a "dead angle" as we say in Japanese.

Miki! Maya called out in a low voice. I have grown near-sighted and astigmatic with old age, but I focused on the spot where she was pointing. There, below the waterfall, I could make out something brown floating in the water. Maya pulled up her pant legs and ran into the water.

Miki was cold and clean after having been sloshed about for several hours in the water. Even though she had fallen the thirty-some feet from the lower portion of the yard into the river, she hardly had a scratch on her. Maya picked up her hard, wet corpse in both arms and carried her back to the house. When we wiped her dry with a bath towel, I realized to my astonishment how light her small body was. It was almost as if her body had become that much lighter when her spirit departed.

I shouldn't have said that to her last night, Maya whispered. I wonder if Miki committed suicide.

You've got to be kidding, I said. Yet at the same time that I denied her theory, I imagined our poor, senile old dog Miki summoning up her last bit of energy to leap over the barricade, totter down the stone stairs to the hidden garden, make her way through the trees, and drag herself to the edge of the precipice. It's hard to imagine that even the most senile of dogs would have stepped over a precipice it knew so well. If not, then perhaps . . .

Several years have gone by since all this happened. Miki died on the eleventh of September, right as a long summer was coming to a close and the autumn wind was just beginning to stir.

Translated by Jeffrey Angles

The Destiny of Shoes

Atōda Takashi

BEYOND THE WINDOW of the bullet train to Kyōto, the cherry blossoms had already fallen; new green leaves now filled the branches. Within the space of ten days, spring had truly arrived.

After Odawara the ocean came into view. The undulating water reflecting the evening light was gray and beginning to grow dark as a mist appeared from the open sea. It would be night by the time the train reached Kyōto.

There were only a few passengers on the train; the seat

The Tōkyō-born writer ATŌDA TAKASHI (1935–) has published over forty volumes of short stories, and in 1979 his short story *Naporeon kyō* (Napoleon Crazy) won the Naoki Prize, one of Japan's most prestigious awards for popular fiction. He has also won several other awards, including the Japan Detective Fiction Society's Award for Short Fiction and the Yoshikawa Eiji Award. He is known for the black humor that often pervades his works. First published in 1981, this story describes an outing to Japan's ancient capital of Kyōto, a major tourist destination, especially when the cherry trees throughout the city are in bloom. Ōhara is a quieter, mountainous location on the northeastern fringes of the city; there one finds several exceptionally beautiful temples built many centuries ago.

next to Ayako had remained unoccupied from the start. She stretched out a leg in front of her and idly swung her foot up and down. She had on blue suede high heels, the same shoes she had worn on her trip only a few days before. Rarely had she taken the bullet train twice within such a short period of time.

"Good-looking shoes." Hadn't the train been passing the same spot when the man in the seat next to her remarked upon her shoes? Now she found it difficult to remember his features clearly. As time passed, it was hard to recall the looks of casual acquaintances. He had been a stocky older man around sixty, the type one might see anywhere. Her impression of him had been generally favorable.

As she absent-mindedly stared out the window she could still picture the characters of the name on his business card: Nakamura Norio. At the time she had wondered why he'd given her his card.

That day when she'd boarded the train at Tōkyō Station a man was sitting in the aisle seat next to hers. He was reading a magazine. She hoped he wouldn't bother her. It is normal for anyone, especially a woman traveling alone, to wish that.

"Excuse me." She edged by him.

"Of course."

She felt reassured as she glanced at his profile. Still, a woman in the next seat would have made her feel more comfortable. When the conductor came to check the tickets she learned that he too was going to Kyōto.

After Yokohama they passed a schoolyard. Its cherry trees were in full bloom and about to scatter. Together they gazed at them. "Beautiful, aren't they?" the man muttered. "The cherries are at their best in Kyōto now too." It was difficult to tell if he was thinking out loud or addressing Ayako.

She nodded vaguely, and the man spoke again. "Are you going to Kyōto for sightseeing?"

"Yes," she replied. She could call it sightseeing since the trip wasn't related to work. "The cherries are in full bloom," Sakuta-san had written her. "How about coming to see them?" Ayako had told him over the phone that she would come see the blossoms. But in reality she was a woman going alone to a place where the man in her life lived. The trip had required a certain amount of resolution. It surely was not the usual pleasure outing.

Ayako had majored in pharmacology in college and was presently working for the National Research Agency. She enjoyed her work, and she had passed thirty before she realized it. Now one could say that Ayako had come to a turning point in her life.

She had met Sakuta Jirō three months ago, and from their first meeting she had felt that their relationship would develop. He was an engineer working for a construction company. His personality seemed to combine two facets of his trade, one as strong as the construction of a dam and the other as sensitive as the craftsmanship of glasswork. The fact that she had analyzed his character to this extent was proof to her of her attraction to him.

She knew that he was married and had a child. It had not been a happy union. Some time had passed since his wife had taken the child and returned to her parents.

"Who's to blame?" she once asked him point-blank. "If

one side was in the wrong," he answered, "we wouldn't have gone on fighting this long."

There was something attractive about the demeanor of this man whose wife had deserted him, and Ayako couldn't find it in her to dislike him. Sakuta had asked her out; Ayako had accepted his invitations. The relationship started off smoothly. Then abruptly Sakuta was transferred to Kyōto, and their meetings came to an unexpected halt.

"Will you visit me?" he'd asked her.

She promised him that she would.

Alone, he proceeded to his new post, and she received a number of letters from him. It appeared that he was very busy with his work, and he wrote that he could not return to Tōkyō for some time.

In that case, she would go to him.

What had prompted her decision? For one thing, spring was in the air, and she was enticed by the urbane fancy of strolling in a new spring outfit through the ancient capital during cherry-blossom season. She particularly wanted to go wearing the Italian suede high heels that had been something of an extravagance for her. The underlying reason for her decision, of course, was her longing to see Sakuta.

Perhaps she was being rash.

There had been no confession of love from him. He was only separated from his wife. Sakuta and Ayako were no more than good friends at the moment. Sooner or later, however, there comes a time in love where one has to risk all. After one turned thirty, there was a certain wisdom in being imprudent.

Once she had decided to see Sakuta, she could find no

reason not to be with him. The way to happiness now was only a matter of buying a train ticket.

There were cherry trees even next to her office building, and the swelling of their buds stirred Ayako's emotions. One Saturday morning she had looked at the branches bright with white blossoms and announced to her supervisor, "I'm taking the afternoon off. There's a memorial service for a relative in the country. I may take Monday too, since I haven't seen the family for a while."

She called Sakuta long distance, told him her plans, then boarded an afternoon train. That was the trip some days back, when the older man sitting next to Ayako had spoken to her.

After they passed Odawara the older man stroked his cheek lightly with a thoughtful expression. "Good-looking shoes," he murmured.

Ayako found this compliment disturbing coming from a stranger. If he had been a younger man she might have felt it distasteful, but somehow his words conveyed an uncommon interest in shoes. He appeared to be genuinely impressed by them.

"They're Italian," Ayako replied with pride. Blue suede was quite common, but that exquisite a shade was rare.

"Casadeis?"

"My, you certainly know your shoes."

"It's my business."

"Oh, I see." Naturally he would have an interest in shoes then, reflected Ayako. She wondered if he was a manufacturer rather than a salesman. His honest manner made her think of a designer more than someone in sales.

"Color is so difficult. To get even a slightly better shade

out of the blues requires that much more technique and that much more money. Even a minute change can mean a major operation."

Feeling at a loss for a reply, Ayako simply nodded.

The man stared intently at her shoes. Although she was uncomfortable, she felt that to move her legs at this point would be insensitive on her part. As she glanced down, her eyes fell on the man's shoes. They were a wine color accented by a brass *G*, a fancy accessory. In comparison to his clothes his shoes were very flashy.

"Do you manufacture shoes?" She tried to change the subject from her own shoes, and she pulled her feet in slightly at the same time.

"Well, yes." The man looked slightly unhappy. "I've made them, and I've sold them." Their conversation ceased for a while. Vendors, young women with rising voices, went up and down the aisle, selling their wares.

As the train came out of a tunnel the man seemed suddenly to remember something important. "Shoes are really very mysterious things," he commented. It was a bizarre remark, yet his manner was entirely serious.

"I beg your pardon?" she asked him.

"I've worked with nothing but shoes for many years and at times I've been quite startled. Funny but I see now that even shoes have something akin to feelings, and I've come to understand them."

"Shoes have feelings?"

"Yes. I guess you could call it the 'voice' of the shoe. At night after I've closed the shop I take a look at the shoes lined up on my shelves. There are always one or two pairs that seem to have something to say. You'll probably laugh, but I'm convinced that shoes have the strength to move the person wearing them. If you end up with shoes with this special power, you never know where they might take you."

It was hard to tell whether he was joking or serious. He was obviously aware of the absurdity of what he was saying, and yet he appeared to be sincere.

"Isn't there a story in the West about a dancer who puts on ballet shoes and begins to dance, and then can't stop? They say she had to keep dancing the rest of her life."

"The Red Shoes." Ayako gave a little laugh. She thought she recognized it as one of Andersen's fairy tales. The combination of a European fairy tale and this middle-aged gentleman seemed so incongruous.

"Oh? I'm not that familiar with the story, but it does prove that the idea has occurred to someone else. For instance, maybe there are some shoes that repeatedly say they have to go abroad, and then the person who wears them actually goes to a foreign country."

"Is that so?"

"There are even ones with loose morals. There's a client of ours from a good, respectable family, but she bought a pair of these strange shoes and, sure enough, she began fooling around with all kinds of men. From the time the shoes were lined up on my shelves they'd been saying they wanted that kind of life. Odd, isn't it?"

"But when the shoes get old, and she gets another pair?" Being the scientist she was, Ayako felt compelled to question his theory.

"Right. But in this girl's case she bought the same kind again and things went from bad to worse."

Indeed, thought Ayako, it did make sense that this was

possible. There could be a certain design that wilder girls would prefer.

The man continued. "Take fashion models. There were many of them among our clients. It's a rough profession with lots of ups and downs. If they're lucky, wealthy men fall for them, and they live in the lap of luxury. On the other hand, those who make just the slightest mistake can turn into prostitutes. I'm not saying they're all like that, but there have been many dragged by their shoes in that direction."

Since his expression remained serious it was impossible to laugh. Ayako shook her head several times as if to snicker. Could it be that shoes went around talking about "living in the lap of luxury" or "becoming a prostitute"? For a story, it was really quite amusing. And yet, because shoes went on the feet, perhaps they *could* take a person somewhere, be the person willing or not.

"The frightening ones are the shoes that want to die."

A sudden chill swept over Ayako. She waited for his next words, but he did not continue. As if half changing the subject and half inquiring further, Ayako smiled and asked, "And my shoes?"

His expression changed to a pleasing grin. "They're fine. There is nothing particularly wrong with them. They're about to run with all their might."

With a start, Ayako looked at the man, who avoided her eyes and turned to another subject. "Are you staying in the city?" he asked.

"Yes, I believe so."

"The blossoms should be good."

"Yes. I was thinking about taking some excursions to see them."

"Try to avoid Arashiyama at all costs. It's full of sightseers. If you go into the hills behind Ōhara, there are some wonderful spots. From Jakkō-in to Mt. Suitai, right around there. There aren't that many trees, but their shapes are quite amazing." So saying, he pulled out a business card from his suit pocket. After pointing out his name, he drew a simple map on the back of the card. "Do try to get there. If you have a car available, it's a great place."

"Thank you." The title on his business card read Managing Director, Nakamura Shoes, Inc.

As the metal catch on her handbag clicked shut it seemed to mark the end of their conversation. After drawing in her feet so that they were out of view, Ayako slept a little. She had not accepted the man's ideas, but the whole conversation had made her feel uneasy, and she did not care to be scrutinized further. The next time she opened her eyes the train was racing alongside Lake Biwa.

Sakuta met her at the station. That night they strolled through the streets of Kyōto together. He had arrived in the metropolis only recently, and he seemed not to know much about this large city or its offshoot environs. He took her to a certain restaurant. "I was told that the food here is good," he said, taking a big bite of fresh bamboo shoots.

"Delicious."

"You really like it?" he questioned.

"Really."

"I don't think the Kyōto nobility ate very well. There's not one good dish in the so-called Kyōto cuisine. It's all form. They've contrived all kinds of spectacles. In the first place, the portions are so small it's pathetic."

"My goodness, can't you think of anything positive to say?"

"Actually, apart from the food, Kyōto has a lot going for it. There's no mistaking that it's culturally superior to Tōkyō. Even a water barrel is made as a work of art. We Kantō barbarians can't touch them here. Their sake is good too."

"You're not drinking that much tonight."

"Maybe not. If I drink too much . . ." Sakuta stopped short.

Ayako finished the sentence for him. "You'll come out with something insincere?"

"No." As is often the case in a man over thirty, a youthful smile lit Sakuta's somber face. "I'm afraid I'll reveal exactly how I feel."

The atmosphere became more relaxed as their conversation loosened up. They got back to her hotel around one in the morning. Sakuta escorted Ayako to the door of her room, where he said good night. "What time shall I be here tomorrow?"

"Whatever time you say is fine with me," she told him. "Don't you sleep late on Sunday?"

"No. How about ten?" he suggested.

"Fine. I'll be ready."

The next day they drove to Sagano. The cherry blossoms were at their height at all the old historical temples—Daikaku-ji, Shaka-dō, Rakushi-sha, Giō-ji. Looking up at a branch full of blooms, Sakuta said, "It looks as if the petals climbed the trees."

Ayako studied his face. Hadn't the ancient nobility used clever words expressing the beauties of nature as a technique of courtship? It was questionable whether Sakuta's unusual way of describing the fullness of the blossoms suited the aesthetic atmosphere, but Ayako was enchanted by it. The cherry-blossom petals overflowed to the ends of each tiny branch and actually looked as if they had vied with each other in climbing up and out to the farthest points of every twig.

"Shall we go on to Arashiyama now that we're here?" he suggested.

"Sounds good," Ayako agreed.

Arashiyama was packed with sightseers. And yet, for Ayako, it differed from the clamor of Tōkyō. The mountain was beginning to grow dark, and in the twilight shadows it was hard to distinguish between the blossoms and the spring mist.

"Where is Ōhara?" Ayako asked. She knew almost nothing about Kyōto.

"It's in an entirely different direction. Absolutely the other side of the city."

"One of the Heike clan members took the tonsure and lived at Jakkō-in, in Ōhara."*

"You mean Kiyomori's daughter, Emperor Antoku's mother."

"A man I met on the train told me there's a quiet grove of cherry trees in the mountains there. He even drew me a map." Ayako opened her bag and brought out the business card.

"It would be a major undertaking to go there now."

"Oh? Then tomorrow?"

---

*The Heike clan, also known as the Taira, was one of four families that dominated politics during the Heian period (794–1185). *(Trans.)*

"Sorry. I've got an important meeting at eleven."

"It doesn't matter. I've seen plenty of blossoms."

"What about going early in the morning?"

"Wouldn't that be too much for you?"

"No. It's not that big a trip. There should be very little traffic at that hour. I'm more concerned about what we'll do now."

"I'm famished."

"Me too. There's nothing but places specializing in tofu dishes around here. How about going back to town for steak and a cup of coffee?"

"Sounds good to me, really splurging."

"Let's go."

"What do you usually do about your meals?" asked Ayako as they returned to the car. Coming from a woman the question might appear slightly forward, she feared.

"All sorts of things," he told her. "Every so often I cook for myself. Do you want to see my place?"

"I'd love to."

The car inched slowly forward on the congested road. It was after seven by the time they reached Sakuta's apartment. There had been no vacancies in company housing, and he had taken a place within the city. The building was a concrete one and more impressive than Ayako had expected.

"I can relax here a lot better than if I were in company housing. And I don't have to worry about the place when I'm away. There seem to be more and more thefts in Kyōto these days."

"Haven't there always been a lot?"

"I'm not really that sure."

"When you read Akutagawa's stories . . ."

"He's before my time." His hunger appeared to be uppermost in his mind. "What do you want to do?"

"I'm tired."

Although it would never pass for a gourmet dinner, fried rice and bachelor's leftovers from the freezer served as supper. They ate at his table, which seated only two. Ayako could find no trace of a woman in his place; there were no signs of a feminine touch. It seemed Sakuta's wife had never visited the place.

Holding a cup of coffee in her hand, Ayako stood by the window and carefully pulled the curtain aside. Dark shapes of mountains were lined up directly beyond the city lights. She was still a little lightheaded from the glass of beer that she had had before dinner.

She wondered why her shoulders trembled when Sakuta touched her from behind, even though she had long anticipated it. Perhaps it was because her expectation had been so accurate. Or was it because there was something to fear?

"Thanks for coming."

"I wanted to see you."

"It looks as if I won't be able to return to Tōkyō for some time. It's been so long since I've had something good in my life. I thought that living outside of Tōkyō wouldn't be so bad, but . . ."

"I understand."

"It's so difficult to get together now." In between words, his lips met hers. His arms slowly tightened around her until he was holding her. The light went out, and a door slid open. It appeared to be the bedroom. With the rough manner of an engineer who works outdoors, he carried her to his bed. Her body rose slightly with the springs.

This was not the first time for Ayako. She had made love with a boy in college, but now that was a distant memory. She closed her eyes, and the semidarkness changed to pitch black. The heat of passion swept her away.

"Beautifully. Beautifully." Why did these words run through her mind? She knew that she wanted to perform beautifully, but beyond that there was an unspoken plea to the man to violate her beautifully.

Then the thought lost its power, and a period followed in which her mind went dizzy with heat. She was aware of his whiteness spreading in her black womb.

She slept a little, but it wasn't a deep sleep. It turned light outside the curtain. What sounded like a handcart passed below. The ancient capital gets up early, she thought. As she turned over, Sakuta awoke. His smiling face bore the faint shadow of a beard, and it filled her with such emotion that she had to look away.

"I wonder what time it is," he said.

"Maybe around four."

"All right then, let's get going."

"Why?" she questioned.

"We're going to Ōhara, aren't we? I want you to see it." He caressed her shoulders and kissed her. The smoldering embers of last night were about to become inflamed again. Sakuta kicked aside the cover to stop himself. If they were going to get to Ōhara, they couldn't waste time.

"Just wash up, and then let's go."

Ayako was good at getting ready quickly. Twenty minutes later the two were dashing out of Sakuta's apartment. The car sped through the waking town, where few people were up and about. They headed north along the Takano River and came to Sanzen-in and Jakkō-in, but it was still too early in the morning for the temple gates to be open. From over the walls they caught only glimpses of monks sweeping the gardens.

Winding up the road, they entered the Mt. Suitai area, exactly as it had been drawn on the back of the business card. Once or twice, Sakuta lost his way, but he continued undaunted. There was a determination about him that made him see things through to the end.

"What we're looking for must be over there," he said. Clusters of white blossoms made the mountain appear speckled.

"I wonder if we can get close to that cliff," Ayako asked.

"We'll get there."

Already everything on the mountain slope was bathed in the morning light. The car coughed along, climbing the rocky incline. Sakuta stopped the car by the side of the road. Looking up at the blossoms, the two walked along a deserted mountain path. Touched by the sunlight, the dew on the flowers glistened brightly.

"Compared to modern times there must have been far fewer colors a long time ago," Sakuta said.

"Maybe that's why they saw the shine of the dew as so extraordinarily beautiful."

"Now with our jewels and neon lights and such we just don't appreciate the simple beauty of nature."

There were even more cherry trees running along the western slope. Ayako took one or two steps along the narrow path through the grass. Then suddenly she stopped.

"What is it?" Sakuta asked.

At first she couldn't answer. She needed time to collect her thoughts. There on the grass in front of her was a pair of men's shoes. She had seen those shoes before. She recognized the wine color, and she recognized the accessory, the letter *G*.

They were his shoes, but why were they here? An answer began to form in her mind. A piece of paper protruded from underneath the shoes. Its message was bizarre. "Please do not be startled. I lie dead beyond you."

Ayako did not look at the body. Sakuta told her that it was hanging from one of the thicker cherry-tree branches and was swinging gently, resembling a *tanzaku* poem-card suspended in the middle of the blossoms.

Some ten days had passed since that time, and Ayako was again on the bullet train headed west. Her feelings had deepened along with the spring. Today too she expected Sakuta to be at the station to meet her. She had read about Nakamura Norio's death in the evening paper. Reportedly his business had failed in Tōkyō, and he had returned to his birthplace to die among the blossoms. It was Saigyō who had written

> Let it be this way
> Under the cherry blossoms,
> A spring death,
> At that second month's midpoint
> When the moon is dull.*

It has been said that people who commit suicide leave behind an attachment to this world, in one form or another. Perhaps the man's writing his place of death on

*Translation quoted from Saigyo, *Mirror for the Moon*, trans. William R. Lafleur (New York: New Directions, 1977). *(Trans.)*

the back of his business card was just that. Perhaps somewhere in his heart he had secretly been waiting for Ayako to rescue him. The memory of his shoes in the grass returned to her. He said that the shoes that wanted to die were the frightening ones. Were his shoes that kind? Once you put them on, was it too late? The man must have simply followed their direction. He had gone to Kyōto, climbed Mt. Suitai, and proceeded to the edge of the precipice as if pulled by a magnet.

She couldn't believe it. When she told Sakuta he laughed lightly. "That's quite a story," he acknowledged.

But now the train speeding through the semidarkness made her feel strangely agitated. It was exactly as if this train were rushing toward something unavoidable.

Ayako glanced down at her feet. As before, she had on the same blue suede high heels. Once again she was headed toward the city where her lover waited, and she felt excited. It was almost as if she too were being pulled or swept along by her shoes.

Perhaps the shoe manufacturer had felt something unusual about her shoes, and yet hadn't told her. Could it be that his silence was due to a premonition of doom? Even if that was true, she did not feel inclined to start all over again.

A man who had been forsaken by his wife was waiting in that beautiful city. Tonight too the two of them would find themselves in a lovers' embrace in that plain apartment. From now on Ayako would undoubtedly be traveling on these tracks over and over again.

What was awaiting her at the end? It wasn't that she had her heart set on happiness. It wasn't that she was hoping against hope to marry Sakuta. Then for what reason was she going? The only thought in her mind was that she had to meet him now. The sound of the train quickened her feelings. Perhaps it was true that her suede shoes were in fact carrying her along. She could hear a faint squeak as she drew her feet together.

Translated by Millicent M. Horton

The Immortal

Nakagami Kenji

TO THE HIJIRI, it was not particularly strange to be pushing his way through a dense thicket as he walked on and on in the mountains of Kumano, thrusting aside the top branches of bushes whose leaves shimmered translucent in the sunlight like blazing fire. That is how he had come this far, walking on and on into the mountains. If Amida were peering down from above the mountains, it may have seemed nothing more than circling round and

NAKAGAMI KENJI (1946–92) is well remembered for his novels about his early life, growing up as a member of the outcast *burakumin* class. His novel *Misaki* (The Cape), which received the Akutagawa Prize in 1976, and *Karekinada* (The Kareki Sea, 1977) are brutal, naturalistic descriptions of the *burakumin* villages in Kumano region of Japan. His later work draws heavily on Japanese and foreign folktales, mythology, and literary theory. This story depicts the popular conception that the deep forests of Kumano are a mysterious, timeless world of ghosts, demons, and other supernatural beings. It also represents a postmodern retelling of Izumi Kyōka's (1873–1939) famous, turn-of-the-century novella *Kōya hijiri* (The Holy Man of Mount Kōya) about the sexual temptation of a *hijiri* (wandering Buddhist monk) who encounters a beautiful, ghostly sorceress deep in the mountains.

round in the same place, sometimes a profile, sometimes a
full figure, like an insect wriggling in the earth beneath the
torn grass. But even if that were true, he did not care in the
least. *Walking suits me.* He had walked on and on reciting
this to himself. And as he walked, he had sometimes
reached the top of a mountain pass to find unexpectedly a
village on the other side. Sometimes, when he had been in
the mountains for a long time, he had suddenly found himself searching for a bamboo grove, wanting to eat something fire had passed through, and wanting to embrace a
woman whose body had warmth. *There are always people
where there's a bamboo grove.* He no longer knew when he
had come to understand this in his bones. To the hijiri, the
sound of wind blowing over bamboo leaves was the sound
of his own throat, the sound of life rising from every pore
of his skin.

The thicket had begun to slope gently upward, but the
hijiri's breathing never became labored, and as he traced
the faint path that remained where people or animals had
trampled the grass, just as he had done up to now, he even
raised his voice imitating the sound of the grass brushing
against his garments . . . *jaarajaara jaarajaara* . . . He had
done nothing to the hair on his face for nearly ten days
now, and his face looked dark and malevolent. His garments, freshly washed ten days ago, had become filthy with
dust and grime. *Jaarajaara jaarajaara* . . . Suddenly, what
had happened ten days ago loomed up before him like a
dream, and the hijiri closed his mouth, swallowing the
sounds. Dense clouds roiled up covering the entire scene.
The gentle slope of the mountain, which had seemed to
melt into the sunlight striking it until just now, the stand

of cypresses spreading out beyond it like outstretched arms, and the naked crags in the distance, to the hijiri's eyes like purple flames, all dimmed, as if their colors had been wiped away. For a moment, the hijiri felt pain bearing down on him. Raising his eyes, he spat loudly, and began to mimic the sound of the grass again . . . *jaarajaara jaara-jaara* . . . as if he were chanting a holy sutra.

He had fasted often, abstaining from both food and drink, and having a devotion to scholarship surpassing that of others, he had been singled out by the person he revered as his master, who had praised him for his speed in learning the sutras. But perhaps because from the very beginning he had learned the sutras only as a child who had been abandoned by hill people, or valley people—or even perhaps by a monkey keeper in favor of the monkey—he always ended up chanting *jaarajaara jaarajaara*, like a lewd growling in the throat, instead of the phrases of the sacred sutras.

Reaching the end of the mountain's gentle slope, he entered a stand of tall cypresses and after walking a little further came out onto the ridge, which was thickly wooded with tall, broad-leaved trees. He walked on, stooping so that the garments covering his large body would not be caught in the branches, and on the ground at his feet, where fallen leaves had piled up and rotted, a snake as thick as his arm slithered away with a rustling sound to hide itself. There were sounds everywhere, like spattering rain-drops—just behind him, something was striking the leaves of the branches over his back. Startled, he whirled around, and then realized that he had stumbled into a nest of mountain leeches. He turned to retreat, but when he tried to brush away the branch hanging over his face, leeches fell from its leaves like gentle raindrops, a great number of them striking his head and tumbling into the collar of his tunic. Shouting out, he twisted his body backward, but the leeches, tiny as the seeds of a tree, stuck to his skin and would not come loose. The hijiri had encountered many such things as he wandered in the mountains. And whenever something like this happened, he was struck with wonder at himself, walking deeper and deeper into the mountains and even going through all sorts of hardships when there was no reason at all to be doing so.

He emerged from the cypress grove onto a precipitous cliff. When he looked down, he could see a swollen waterfall that seemed to rend the rocks, and a river. Catching the sunlight, the water shimmered like white silk, and the hijiri felt that even from a distance its beauty was breathtaking. He wanted desperately to dip out some of this water and drink it, and unable to contain himself, he began searching for a way down. After nearly an hour, he finally reached the bottom of the cliff. First, as if it were a perfectly natural thing to do, he thrust his face directly into the water and drank, kneeling on a moss-grown rock that received the spray of the waterfall. He drank with such force as to gulp down everything in the river into his stomach. When he had finally finished drinking, he washed his face and then his head in the water. Suddenly, as if it had just occurred to him, he plunged splashing into the swift current with all his clothes still on. Standing in water up to his hips, he washed his flanks, his neck, and his back, which were covered with marks where the leeches had sucked his blood. He had stopped the bleeding by covering the wounds with crushed blades of grass, and now the scabs softened and came loose in the water. Blood flowed from the wounds, seeming to dissolve instantly in the water. The hijiri was not surprised by a little blood. Perhaps because he had been in a village ten days earlier, he was fleshier than usual.

The hijiri walked through the water toward the water-fall, which shone with a white radiance like a length of silk. Reaching the base of the cascade, it occurred to him that if he was going to be beaten by this strand of silk, he would profit more naked than with his clothes on, and so he began to take off his wet garments. Just at that moment he heard a sound and whirled around. For an instant the hijiri doubted his own eyes.

Separated by the cliff from where he stood, a woman was dipping water from the river with a bamboo ladle into a wooden bucket. He wondered suspiciously what she was doing here, where there was not the slightest sign of a vil-lage, but rather than startle her by making a sound, he watched the weak movements of the woman's hands, bat-ing his breath. She filled the dipper half-full, but appar-ently it was too heavy for her and she spilled the water. She plunged the dipper into the water again. He saw the ladle floating weakly on the surface, but it was only after the woman cried out and began running downstream along the bank that he realized it had been captured by the swift current.

The dipper was carried down to his feet, and when the woman realized that a hijiri was bathing himself in the small waterfall that plunged into the river, she turned her face away. The hijiri understood what the woman standing before him felt. Fear at having stumbled upon a man deep in the mountains, an ascetic attempting to purify his body in the descending torrent, was clearly visible on her face.

Picking up the dipper, the hijiri straightened his garments and walked through the water toward the trembling woman. Her hair was neatly gathered at the nape of her neck, and the white ankles he glimpsed beneath the hem of her kimono were slender. That alone was enough to evoke from the hijiri's throat the sound of grass rustling, the sound of treetops brushing against each other in the wind . . . *jaarajaara jaarajaara*. Slowly, he stopped in front of the woman, muttering that even a scholar-priest bound by high rank at the main temple would violate the commandments if he met a woman alone in the mountains.

The woman raised her face and looked at the hijiri, but now there was neither pleading nor fear in her expression. When the hijiri peered into the reflection of himself in her large eyes, there was even a suggestion of a faint smile playing on her white face. "Thank you," she said, reaching out to take the bamboo dipper. Her hands were too small for her body, as if they had remained unchanged since she was an child. Staring intently into his face as if to confirm that his excited lust had faltered, the woman took the dipper in her tiny hands and said, "You must forget this." And then she began to climb quickly up into the brush on the mountainside, leaving the half-filled bucket where it had fallen beside the river.

For a moment, the hijiri stood rooted there as if in a trance. But after the woman's figure disappeared into the thicket, it occurred to him suddenly that she had not been a creature of this world. If she were a flesh-and-blood woman, he could rape her. But if she were an incarnation of Kannon, he could save himself from this existence if he but touched her gentle, infant's hands—this existence as a hijiri who could not live in the villages of men but neither was able to devote himself to scholarship. He plunged into the under-growth after her, then paused to listen, and heard birds taking flight in the distance. He set off in the direction of this sound, without a thought for his soaked garments.

When he emerged from the thicket, the woman was kneeling beside a flat brushwood fence. The hijiri ran up behind her and stopped, standing over her. "Please leave me alone." Her weak, pleading voice seemed to emerge from her lips in a single thread, as if she sensed his rising passion. Here deep in the mountains, she could have escaped had she tried, and even as he lifted the cowering woman in his arms, the hijiri could not suppress the feeling that he was being deluded, though she closed her eyes and weakly gave herself up to him.

Exposing her naked body, he was both disappointed and relieved to find that apart from her hands there was no sign that she was more than human.

After he had sated his passion, he asked her why she was gathering water alone in the mountains, and if she lived here with her husband. But the woman with the infant's hands only wept silently. He helped her up, but she closed her kimono and said only, "Please, just leave me as I am." The hijiri wondered if she was living alone here because of her stunted hands, to avoid inquisitive stares.

He had no intention of letting the woman go. The grass where she had sunk down was soft and gentle, and the hijiri thought it suited her white thighs. Drawn by their white-ness, he reached out to touch them, but she brushed his hand away, twisting her body back, and said, "Please leave me alone."

The sun was still in the sky but already turning red. When he lunged at her, the woman raised her arms to embrace him, pulling him down with her tiny hands. He thought that to a woman he must appear to be unimaginably crazed, and buried his face in her breasts, pressing his lips against her nipples and biting them lightly. Perhaps because this hurt her, the woman pressed her lips against his and sucked his tongue into her mouth. Just at that moment, he heard low voices around them. He tried to raise his head, but the woman held it down with her tiny hands and said, "Wild boars often pass by here." Not satisfied with this, he again tried to raise his head in search of the voices, but she pressed her body up against his and wrapped her legs around him. "It's only the cries of boar or deer running past toward the ridge."

When she insisted again, the voices did sound like animal cries. But deep in the mountains, with darkness suddenly falling over everything, the hijiri felt approaching danger. He sensed someone standing behind him and whirled around, but the woman wrapped her arms more tightly around his neck to stop him and said, "It is the noble ones." The hijiri threw off her arms and stood up, staring intently into the gloom.

The light that had lingered in the sky until moments before had begun to disappear, the mountains fading into nothing but shifting shadows, so he could not make out their features, but with sounds like the wind rustling in the brush, they were gathering one or two at a time to sit before him. For a moment, he thought he saw their faces, and he felt fear stabbing up from the pit of his stomach—*yasha*, night demons. Trembling, he pushed the woman away, and clutching his garments tried to run away. But the woman—where did she find the strength?—seized his hand in her own infant's hands and stood up facing him. "Do not be afraid," she whispered. "No one thinks you are a savage like Ise no Gorō." The hijiri had no idea what this meant, but she had drawn nearer, and so he shouted out to the crowd hidden in the darkness, "I am nothing like that," trying to tell them that he was only an ascetic who had happened to pass by this place in his wanderings.

"I won't bother you. I haven't even seen your faces."

From the darkness came voices that sounded like scornful laughter.

"I haven't seen anything. I don't know anything." He was shouting, but when he heard laughter in what were clearly human voices—had he said something funny?—the hijiri suddenly realized that he was shaking. *What am I doing standing here frightened out of my wits and trying to make excuses for myself?* The hijiri saw himself for the first time naked and shaking, unable even to throw off the grip of the woman's tiny hands. He had valued his own life no more than that of an insect. He had gone down into the villages, and claiming to be a seer with long years of austerities, had wandered from place to place curing nightmares, performing exorcisms, and even telling fortunes. Sometimes, he had stolen the handful of rice that was all a family possessed. Once, when he had left the villages to wander again in the mountains, he had encountered rain, and before he could descend from the peak he had become feverish. But thinking that he had no need of life, he had simply fallen down against the base of a tree and lain there until the fever passed by itself. The hijiri laughed at himself. He, who had thought there was no particular reason to live, was now trembling in fear that his life might be taken by these yasha devils.

"It is the noble ones."

The woman took the garments from his hands and put them on him. And then, as if they had been waiting for her to finish, they all began to walk, making a rustling sound in the brush.

"Come, let's be off," the woman said, taking the hijiri's hand. She started walking, and the clumps of grass around him moved. He heard the sound of many feet trampling the grass.

He did not know how long they walked. It seemed they arrived almost at once, but also that several hours had passed. Though he had wandered endlessly here, the hijiri knew only that they were deep in the mountains, far from the villages that dotted the seacoast. He had no memory of the steep slope they were climbing or of the shape of the mountain that loomed up in the moon he glimpsed hanging in the sky whenever there was a break in the trees. They came to a place where he could hear the sound of spray, and a soft, cold mist struck his face, and he knew they were near a waterfall. "Just a little further now," she whispered in his ear. And as she had promised, they emerged from the grove of trees onto a broad, flat river-bank that opened before them in moonlight, which now covered the entire scene, and above it was a waterfall that plunged down from the heights with the sound of bells, aglow in the silver light. Next to the fall was a mansion, its lights so dim that it seemed uncertain whether it was actually there at all.

"The waterfall turns red, like flowing blood."

As if to show him, she pointed to the waterfall, which was drenched in the light of the moon. He heard a harsh, suppressed voice beside him:

"Have we not sworn revenge on the traitors of Tanabe?"

Voices of agreement rose all around him—"Yes" . . . "Indeed" . . . Just then, a person of small stature appeared from the mansion holding two birds in his hands. Knocking the shrieking, flapping birds against each other, he shouted, "There, fight once more." Each time they were knocked together, the two birds kicked their legs out at each other and beat their wings, as if they were terrified of the impenetrable night.

The birds were brought together again and again, until finally one of them lost its strength and was no longer able to kick back at the other.

Apparently there was someone of noble birth inside the mansion, for the little man held the birds up toward it. In the silver light of the moon, which just at that moment hung directly overhead, their blood flowed black.

The voice of a woman weeping inside the mansion reached his ears. The little princess had been put to the sword, she said, and she herself had been forced to flee with the prince, who once had been promised the royal succession. Now they were reduced to living here in hiding deep in the mountains. These people, gathered under the cover of night—how many were there?—were only waiting for the right moment to rise up and attack in force. She spoke as though the capital were just on the other side of the mountain.

A soft, warm breeze was blowing. And with each gust the sound of the brush and the tops of the trees echoed like court music played by noble ladies-in-waiting. As if summoned by the voice of the woman crying inside the mansion, they assembled, pushing through the brush with the same mournful, haunting sound. Suddenly recalling the woman at his side, the hijiri looked at her face. Tears glittered in her eyes. He turned again to look at the people assembled in the silver moonlight and shuddered. Their outlines were hazy, and they could easily have been mistaken for the grass, or the branches of the trees, now only shadows in the darkness, but if he looked at them more intently, they were monkeys and wild boars. Yet they all had the shapes of human beings, no different from the hijiri himself. Some had human faces but the hands and feet of dogs. Whether they had become this way from being in the mountains for so long, or because the nobles living in the mansion had assembled a horde of yasha and devils, they were all weeping at the words of the woman inside. Some of them crouched with their hands together in prayer. Others stood covering their faces with hoofed hands. As he gazed at these creatures, the hijiri thought that it was because such things occurred deep in the mountains of Kumano that the hijiri and bikuni who wandered from province to province longed for and worshiped this land. He did not think that these weird monsters were phantoms. And neither did he believe they were the ghosts of the dead who had been defeated and had fled from the capital in this world. They were here now—the infant emperor who had been carried to the bottom of the ocean, and the slain princess whose blood stained the waterfall red.

When the hijiri stood up to leave, the woman with the tiny hands lifted her tear-streaked face and asked, "Where will you go?" In his heart, the hijiri replied that he had had nowhere to go from the beginning, that there was nothing for him but to keep going on and on, but he did not give voice to these thoughts and simply started walking. He sensed that the woman had risen and was following after him with weak, uncertain steps. *If you are some incarnation that is more than human, stay here and cry*, he thought. He was still immature, unfinished, and despite his wanderings and his austerities he could not yet perform feats like En no Gyōja, manipulating devils and flying freely through the air. Even if he had been beaten by waterfalls and denied himself the five grains, none of it had been more than empty ritual.

Listening to the footsteps of the woman following him, he knew that sounds *jaarajaara jaarajaara* were rising around her. Were they made by the deformed creatures standing behind her, or was it just the wind blowing over the treetops?

He did not know the reason, but he felt ashamed. Unable as he was to live among other people, and at the same time wanting in his devotion to austerities, he nevertheless had an ordinary human body, unlike this woman and her monstrous companions. He could not accustom himself to life in the villages, and he was also incapable of true austerity. He knew that the woman was following him closely so as not to lose sight of him, and the sounds *jaara-jaara jaarajaara* rose up even louder in his heart as he traced his way back through the brush from which they had originally come.

The rim of the mountain began to glow, and the hijiri stopped and turned back to the woman.

"Where are you going?"

She smiled and said, "I will see you on your way and then return to the noble ones. That is the way I live."

They had come to a place where the mountain jutted out to form a cliff, and so the hijiri sat down. The woman came up beside him.

"I no longer know how many years I have lived. The noble one mourns her lost children so. There it is."

Peering down from the cliff, she pointed with one of her childlike fingers. The wind blew through her hair, and to the hijiri her face was more lovely than anything he had ever seen before. He found himself looking down from the precipice, as if captivated by her gaze. It was there that he had suddenly wanted desperately to drink from the waterfall, and there that he had been inspired to enter the falls and be lashed by the cascading water. The morning sun had begun to rise, and the rim of the mountain sparkled in golden light. As if night had suddenly become afternoon, birds began to cry out all over the mountain, and the sound of the water reached his ears.

He began to climb down toward the waterfall. Suddenly, he thought that he had seen this thicket before. And it was then that the hijiri realized that the stand of tall, broad-leaved trees he had walked through with the woman during the night was the place where he had been attacked

by leeches. It seemed strange now that nothing in particular had happened to them.

As he climbed down through the brush the sound of the
water pealing in the cold morning air and the woman's
footsteps merged with the sounds *jaarajaara jaarajaara* that
had begun to rise up again in his body, buzzing in his
throat. He emerged from the brush and turned to help the
woman, who had climbed down after him. Taking her into
his arms, he lowered her from the mountainside and without releasing her laid her down beside the stream.

In the bright morning light streaming down on the
riverbank, her naked body breathed colors of peach blossoms, and the downy hair that lightly covered her skin
seemed aglow with the color of gold. As if to kneel before
this beauty, the hijiri lowered his head and pressed his lips
against her skin. He pressed his ear into the valley between
her breasts, and the rapid beating of her heart assured him
of the woman's arousal. He stripped off the garments he
was wearing and stretched his body out beside her. It was
enough to do nothing, enough that this woman was there
breathing beside him, with her skin of peach blossoms
bathed in morning light and her golden down—her red
nipples, her navel, which seemed to him the center of this
world, the burning shadow of her vagina, and the thicket
of hair over it. Not resisting the touch of his lips, the
woman opened her legs to the kneeling hijiri and gently
stroked his back with her tiny hands. He took the fingers
of those hands into his mouth, sucking them one at a time.
The woman raised her hips to accept his engorged penis,
and pressed her lips over his. He plunged into her, as if by

doing so he were arresting the flight of an angel in a feathered mantle, holding her here.

The woman came forth again and again, and with her hands clutching his back, the hijiri thought she was too beautiful in the glaring light of the morning sun. *I don't want to let her go*, he thought. If she was an angel, he wanted to hide away the feathered robe that would carry her to heaven and stay here coupled with her like this forever.

After he too had come forth inside her and the vortex of passion within him had passed, he put his hand on her, and with his fingers stopped the semen that had collected inside and was beginning to flow out. "Stay with me like this forever," he said. The woman smiled, slowly shook her head, and stood up. She said that she would wash herself in the river, and began to walk toward it. As he watched her retreating back, the hijiri was seized with an evil thought. Chanting *jaarajaara jaarajaara*, the meaningless sounds with their lewd reverberations that he chanted instead of the words of the sutras, he saw a vivid image of himself wandering from village to village, from mountain to mountain, like a beggar or a thief, and he thought, *Shall I . . . jaarajaara . . . kill this woman?*—just as the hijiri he saw in his mind, unable to bear his own existence, had once killed a woman. He could see the semen that he had ejaculated into her flowing out and falling onto the sand. As if quite unaware that the hijiri staring at her back was contemplating something abominable, the woman piled her hair up on her head and stepped into the cold water.

The hijiri suddenly felt that the woman was about to disappear completely into the river and stood up to run after her. Looking up at the hijiri, who had come splashing through the current to stand beside her, she smiled and said, "The water is cold." He watched her plunge head first into the water with the same evil feelings and murmured to himself, *She is like the spirit of the morning soaking into your skin.* He splashed her, like a child playing, but she just smiled, not joining in his play. Her demure manner made him uneasy, and his expression became serious.

"Come live with me in a village or somewhere. Who cares about the noble ones? Let's go to a village and plant fields and rice paddies. I can exorcise the children's night demons, and I can make medicines for boils and sicknesses of the mind and sell them."

"I cannot go to a village where there are people."

"If you don't want to go to a village, here in these mountains is fine. I could hunt boar or deer."

The hijiri approached the woman, who was covering her breasts with her infant's hands, and embraced her. He felt it unbearably sad that her skin had been chilled by the cold water, and hugging her more tightly, he thought he was going to cry.

"Stay with me. Live with me. . . ." He knew how rash his proposal was. Whatever her circumstances, she must have some reason for being in such a place, and she knew no more about him than he knew about her. The hijiri felt that even now she might disappear from his arms, and put even more strength into them, pressing his stomach against her wet nakedness. His lips on the nape of her neck, he groaned, "Won't you save me?" He knelt in the water and kissed her breasts, pressing his lips between her fingers. She responded to his caresses, removing her tiny hands.

Lifting her in his arms, the hijiri walked toward the garments he had thrown from the stream. Perhaps because he had walked through the night, the roar of the waterfall echoed in his ears, seeming to spread out behind him, and the voices of the birds, more and more of them as the sun spread over the mountain, sounded clear and strong.

He could not suppress his rising passion—it was as if he had not yet embraced her even once. He put her down on a flat rock at the edge of the stream, and not even giving her time to warm herself, spread her taut pink thighs and entered her, unconcerned that the woman was arching her back in pain. But her pain passed quickly, turning to pleasure. She opened her mouth and stuck out her tongue for his and sucked it into her mouth. When he thrust his hips forward like a rutting boar, she closed her eyes and moved her tongue teasingly, as if to say that only she was giving pleasure. He felt himself an animal possessed of nothing but lust. And he thought himself incomparably repulsive.

He looked down at the woman, who had closed her eyes into gentle lines and released her coiling tongue, moaning in her ecstasy. He felt a hatred welling up that was equal to the love seething in his body. Still rutting like a boar, he grabbed her shoulders and butted into her again and again, grunting out loud. The woman just moaned. He knew that he had put his hand on her throat.

Certainly, he contemplated killing her. He put more strength into the hand he had pressed against her neck, and her body stiffened. He felt her vagina tighten hard around him and mounted higher, trying to thrust more deeply into

her. The woman writhed in pain. He took his hand away
from her throat. He thought he had understood everything from the beginning, and, still naked, he lifted himself off her and sat staring down at her body. She was
watching his face. With the morning sun striking them,
the stream, the rocks, and the woman's naked body were
almost blinding. The brush beside the stream rustled in
every gust of wind, and though the sound did not reach his
ears, he thought he could hear *jaarajaara jaarajaara*. And
though the woman by no means said any such thing, he
imagined that he heard her tiny voice saying, "Please let me
go. . . . Spare my life"—just as he had heard when he killed
the woman in the village. She had known he was little
more than a thief and a beggar, but every night the village
woman had called him "Holy man . . . reverend priest."
And when she called him that, he could not bear it. When
she called him that, he thought that however much he had
fallen, he was still a hijiri, and in fact he had even begun to
convince himself that his incarnation as a hijiri was only
temporary, that he was really a holy saint, in no way inferior to Kōbō Daishi or Ippen Shōnin. *But it was a lie. I am
inferior even to the grass, inferior even to a wild dog, a man
who cannot live in the villages with other people, but who lacks
the wisdom to become a scholar-priest. When she nestled her
cheek against me and kissed me as if she were receiving it with
a reverence that went all the way down to the toes of her feet,
when she worshiped me that way, I felt as if I were being
mocked, tormented, as if I were being gently strangled with silk
floss. And in the darkness of the night, she cried out to me endlessly: "Ah! Save me! . . . Give me salvation! . . . Teach me the
way! . . ." She moaned. She trembled. She threw herself on me*

as if I were the personification of all that was evil and without mercy, groveling and begging for salvation. And sometimes I felt that her voice was my own voice. I was pleading to myself for salvation and at the same time saying the same words in my heart to the woman: "Ah! Teach me! . . . Save me! . . . Teach me the path to paradise! . . ." From early morning that day, I sat in her house with the rain shutters closed, listening to the cries of a cuckoo. As I fondled her dusky nipples while she lay sound asleep beside me, I remember that I thought its cries sounded like "ako, ako, ako. . . ." I rolled her nipple around in my fingers for a moment, and then, just as I had done long, long ago, I sucked it into my mouth. She cried out to me again, "Ah! Holy saint! . . ." The rain shutters were closed, and so I couldn't see her face, but the cries of the cuckoo echoed, "ako . . . ako . . . ako. . . ." "Ah, holy man . . . reverend priest . . . Save me. . . . Save me. . . ." Her cries became louder, and with her moaning in my ears, my hand stretched out toward her throat. Save me. . . . I was saying it with her as I put more strength into my hand. "Save me. . . ." Even after I had released her limp body, her voice remained in my ears forever.

The hijiri had said nothing to the woman.

His body empty, he stood up, and, with the sound of the treetops fluttering *jaarajaara jaarajaara* in his ears, he began to walk toward his garments to put them on. But suddenly he changed his mind and turned toward the water. He stepped into it and then dived, submerging himself. Standing up again, he started to walk toward the waterfall, wiping away the drops of water on his skin with his hands.

Gazing up at the white cascade shooting bright rays of light in the sun, he felt that it was the same waterfall he had seen beside the mansion of the noble ones. It occurred to him that soon it should be stained red with blood, and he turned back to ask the woman with the infant's hands. But from somewhere a great flock of crows had gathered around her, as if to conceal her from him. They had come down near the spot where he had left his clothes and were now hopping around and flapping their wings on the flat ground near the river. Afraid that they would peck the woman's body, he scooped up a rock from the bottom of the river and threw it at them. One by one, they flew up, and squawking loudly to each other, circled over his head.

The hijiri finished putting on his clothes and turned to ask the woman one last time if she would live with him in a village. There was no one there. The hijiri thought he had known that from the beginning, too.

Translated by Mark Harbison

One Night with Mother

Mizukami Tsutomu

SEVERAL MONTHS HAVE PASSED since my mother died on the fifteenth of February. A hint of winter is now in the air, bringing back a vivid memory of the freezing, snowy day we held her burial service. Unlike my brother and sister, who spent much more time with her, I had lived away from Mother since I was nine, so I have not quite been able to grasp the reality of her death. I sometimes feel that she is still alive back in Wakasa, in Fukui Prefecture. It is often said that people can stand on their own two feet only after their parents pass away. People sometimes say

MIZUKAMI TSUTOMU (1919–2004)—also sometimes known as Minakami Tsutomu, due to a common mistake in reading the Kanji characters in his name—had an extremely prolific career as an author of popular fiction. Born in the rural mountains of Fukui Prefecture located near the Sea of Japan, he often depicted the landscapes, sights, and sounds of that region. His works range from mysteries to novels about social problems. Several of his novels, including *Gan no tera* (The Temple of Wild Geese, 1961) and *Echizen take ningyō* (The Bamboo Doll from Echizen, 1963) have become classics of modern Japanese popular fiction. Mizukami first published this essay about his mother in 1981.

they see the images of their mothers and fathers in the mountains and rivers even when they are far away from home. I understand that feeling, but the place where I imagine Mother to be is in that small house in the mountains of Wakasa. Some part of me wants to believe that she is still sleeping there.

I went home to Wakasa for each of the services commemorating her death: the service on the seventh day, on the forty-ninth day, and again on the one-hundredth day. Whenever I go home I see how the lives of my brother and his wife have changed in that house without Mother. Yet as soon as I return to Tōkyō the vision of them alone is supplanted with a vision of the house with Mother in it, and I realize her death has not yet struck me as real. How odd that is! Speaking of strange things, the images of Mother that come to mind when I tell others about her are only from certain periods, even though she lived to be eighty-two years old. The images are vivid but disconnected fragments of her life, like pages from a daily calendar that someone forgot to tear off.

This is only natural: I left home when I was nine, went back home when I fell ill at twenty, and left again two years later when I got better. After that, I spent only a few days at a time with Mother whenever I went home to take care of things. For that reason my images of Mother are mostly from before I left home at the age of nine. In the days before my departure she was still a young and lively woman in her prime. That was because she had me when she was twenty-one; she wasn't even thirty years old when I left. While my brother and his wife probably imagine Mother in her fifties, sixties, or even older, I have no such memories of her. For that reason there have been moments when I listen to others talk about her old age, and I lapse into silence, realizing the gap between their mental images of her and mine.

It was probably when I was eight or so—shortly before I was sent to a temple in Kyōto to become a monk-in-training. My elder brother was ten, the younger one was two, and my other brother and sister had not yet been born. Since we had no bath at home, we would go to other people's houses in the village and ask them if we could bathe there. Earlier in the evening we would check the smoke coming out of the chimneys to see which houses were boiling water for a bath that night. Then we would go there later. We usually visited the families on Mother's side. Since we were walking the roads at night, we took a paper lantern. The roads were stony, and I was in charge of holding the lantern and walking a couple of steps before my mother, who carried my younger brother on her back.

Before we left home, Mother would call for the lantern. First, I would take the lantern down from the pillar where it hung. It was made of a lattice of thin bamboo sticks and oiled paper and was attached to the end of a long, thin handle. An iron chain was attached to the bottom of the lantern, and the other end of it was connected to the tip of the handle. To reach the candle inside, I would have to fold back the oil paper. At Mother's request I would look for a match, light the wick inside the lantern, and then close the lantern by putting the oil paper back and fastening it with a latch. Because I was able to monopolize the matches in those moments, I suddenly felt like a grownup—older than my elder brother, who was two years my senior. I loved smelling the aroma of the melting wax and the oil paper as it warmed up.

Once we got outside we walked down a slope. Soon we approached some streams and crossed countless small bridges. On a snowy day it took us about twenty minutes to reach our destination. I walked in front. Because my role was to light the path for Mother behind me, I was not supposed to walk too fast. Whenever I sped up too much, mother would call out to me to stop, shouting in a high-pitched voice, "Wait, wait!"

In response, I would hold up the lantern over my head and light the road behind me. The snowy paths were slippery, and mother walked slowly because of her high wooden clogs. She bought rubber boots for her children but not for herself. She used to wear a pair of *monpe* work pants—or what were called *karusan* in the Wakasa region. They were red pants with a floral pattern. She wore the wider ones— the kind younger people wore—and because she rolled up the pant legs, four inches or so of her ankles showed. Where her skin was exposed, it was fleshy and pale.

I particularly remember one evening in May or June when, as usual, we were on our way to take a bath at someone's house. While I was guiding my family, lantern held high, Mother stopped me. "Give me the lantern for a minute." I turned around and gave it to her. She held it over the surface of the stream and examined the water closely. That was where the stream bent and the water became almost three feet wide, running parallel to the stony path we were on. At a certain point there were stone steps that led to a spot where people would wash rice and do laundry. Those spots were known as *kawato*; some were shared by neighboring households, and others were used as a private wash places. I wonder if the word is written with a combination of the characters meaning "river" and "door." Even today I am not sure since I have never seen the word written.

Mother took the lantern from me and stepped down the stone steps with my little brother who was sleeping on her back. As she stood at the edge of a foundation stone by the water, her white ankles and calves seemed to glow in the dark.

Holding up the lantern, she shed light onto the stream and circled it over the water. She seemed to be looking for something. Tilting the lantern slightly so that the bottom of it would not cast a shadow, she moved it just above the water, lighting up an area about the diameter of an oil-paper umbrella.

Mother remarked in a cheerful but low voice: "Look at all the *zugani*!"

Zugani is a kind of crab that lives in rivers. Mother had a naturally high-pitched voice, but she would use a lower register when she was being humorous. Enticed by her voice, I walked stealthily down the steps and stood next to her. I heard the sound of the brook flowing somewhere far away, but the current at the *kawato* was rather slow. Because of a small dam only a yard downstream, there was a gentle, swirling eddy. I noticed pebbles, scraps of vegetables, and junk metal at the bottom of the stream. I stared at the images of these small objects as they passed through the transparent water forming a mass of orange light. In the darkness the lantern's light flickered at the bottom of the stream, making it look like the entire bottom of the stream was moving.

I noticed two crabs on a small rock close to me. One was about the size of my fist. It stayed still, its black, hairy legs spread wide. The other one was slightly smaller, but its shell and legs were the same color as the other one. The second one was sitting very close to the big one, almost clinging to its mate.

"Look, that's their nest."

Mother swung the lantern further away. Now I saw small caves on the other side of the stream. Wherever there was a gap at the bottom of the stone wall, the crabs had hollowed out a small cave the size of my fist.

I asked her, "Do they live in those?"

Mother said, "A daddy crab and mommy crab live in each one."

That was when I learned that crabs had the habit of looking for food only at night. But because I was young, those two black crabs clinging to each other just looked like they were fighting.

"Why don't you bring some worms tomorrow and catch them?"

Mother glanced at the crabs still clinging to each other by their legs, then she swung the lantern away from the spot. After she stepped up the stone steps to the *kawato*, she gave me the lantern, telling me to hurry and guide everyone to our relatives' house.

Mother taught me how to catch crabs. She showed me how to punch a small hole in a piece of straw, put two worms halfway inside, and close the straw so that the worms would stay stuck in the hole. We would go back to the spot where we had seen a crabs' nest the previous night then float the straw at the mouth of the nest to entice the

crabs out of the nest. Here's the way it worked. The day
after finding the crabs by the *kawato*, she told me to come
with her to the rice paddy where she grew rice as a tenant
farmer. Before we left home she took a few sturdy pieces
from a bundle of straw. She cleverly broke off the straws at
a joint, pulling the husk from the joint to expose the core
of the straw. Next, she flattened the core by pulling it
between her thumb and index finger, then punched a hole
with a fingernail. After preparing the straw, we took it to
a rice paddy. Mother walked on one of the ridges between
the rice fields. When she got to the gate irrigating the paddies, she squatted down and turned over a straw mat. At
the gate, which was called a *mito*, there was a ridge lower
than the rest of the rice field. Earlier, she had placed the
straw mats at the gate to prevent the soil from being
washed away. Mother turned over one of the mats, exposing the creased surface of the soil underneath. There were
about twenty worms squirming around, all wriggling
because the mat was suddenly gone. Mother picked a few
worms, each about the size of a toothpick, and thrust them
halfway into the hole in the core of the straw then pulled
the straw husk back down to wedge them in the hole. Since
the hole in the straw squeezed their bellies, the worms
were now squirming frantically. They stretched and curled
their heads and tails to and fro.

Mother carried the straw back to the village, and
together we returned to the spot at the *kawato* where we
had discovered the nest of crabs. Mother took off her *zōri*
sandals and walked into the stream. She rolled her work
pants up to her knees with one hand. To get rid of the
bunched-up layers around her thighs, she hoisted up her

upper kimono, which had been tucked inside her pants. I could see the edge of her underwear peeking through a slit on the side of her pants. Mother had slight underarm odor; I could smell its sweet and sour scent when I got close to her. Because the crab's nest was deep inside the cave, I could not see anything. Mother held the straw with the worms wedged in it and let it float at the entrance of the hollow. Once the worms were thrust into the water, they started moving their heads and tails vigorously. Mother pushed the worms just inside the hollow. Suddenly, she felt something and quickly pulled the straw up to examine the worms. One of the worms had been bitten off halfway.

"See, there they are. Do what I just did. You try it now."

She explained that the crabs were now anxious to leave the nest to get the food that had just been snatched away. She told me to move the straw with the worms to the mouth of the nest, assuring me the crabs would come out if I did it just the way she did. As I switched positions with Mother to get to the spot where she was squatting in the water with her white calves exposed, I felt her hand on my back. I put the worms in the water just as she had.

Mother was observing my performance from behind, where she stood in the water. Again, I noticed her plump calves. Her ankles looked thick and short underwater.

It took a long time before a crab poked its legs out of the tiny cave. After all, they are highly cautious, nocturnal creatures. At first, it would touch the worms with only the tip of its sharp leg. Then it gradually extended its legs and tried touching the worms with a couple of legs simultaneously. At that point, I pulled the straw closer to me. Reaching for the food, the crab exposed its hairy legs up to the second joints. Earlier, when I had made noises, the crabs quickly withdrew into the nest and refused to show their legs, so when this one finally felt comfortable enough to show its claws, I was excited.

Mother said, "It's out! It's out!"

Hearing Mother's voice, the crab withdrew and would not come out again.

"Just be patient and keep trying. It'll come out." She walked up the path, sighing as if tired of playing with me—despite the fact that she was the one who had taught me this game. "I'm going back to the rice field," she said, and she walked away, leaving me behind in the stream.

I shifted my gaze from the hole with the crabs to my mother. Her wide hips undulated to both sides as she walked. She had the habit of extending her arms back slightly. She also walked quickly, almost as if she were running. As she walked swiftly away, her breasts bobbed forward.

It was fun to have Mother teach me things. To be honest, I was not terribly interested in catching crabs, so when Mother left I felt lonely. I ran from the *kawato* to the street, leaving behind the straw and worms at the crab's nest. I ran after Mother.

"Mama! Wait!" I seem to recall crying out to her, but I am not sure if I did or not. Mother was walking too fast for a young child like me to catch up, no matter how fast I ran. For some reason, Mother left me behind.

Why did Mother take me to the village stream and teach me to catch crabs? That was May or June, a time we should have been busy weeding the rice fields. Or was it as late as July? I am not certain. Anyway, even to this day, I do not know why she wanted to teach me to catch crabs. Nor do I know why Mother refused to take me to the rice paddy even though I always longed to spend time with her.

The field did not belong to her. She was a tenant who grew rice for someone else, and that person gave her a portion of the rice as a reward for her labor. That was how she raised her children. Father was rarely home. Whenever I asked about him, Mother simply said, "He's in the city." She would never tell me where he went. Whenever he started working at a new construction site, he would not come home for months. He would stay at the onsite bunkhouse. In the prime of her womanhood, around the age of thirty, Mother spent most of her nights alone with us, but during the daytime, she worked hard in someone else's rice field, rarely allowing her children to come to the paddy. And yet, I would still long to run after her and visit her there.

Mother's rice field was located deep in the narrow valley between two hills. It was a kind of rice paddy called *shiru tanbo*, or a "muddy rice paddy," built in staircase fashion on hilly terrain. I walked stealthily to the valley and made my way up to the rice paddies. As I walked up the steep side of the valley, each paddy became narrower; it looked as if they were stacked on top of one another like terraces. The green ears of rice bent before the wind like waves.

Mother was in the middle of the green ears of rice, all by herself. She was submerged in the muddy field to her navel. She was motionless as she faced the other way. With her back rounded, she looked downward into the green of the field. If I had looked more closely, I would have seen her turning the soil with a three-pronged hoe, but to me it looked like she was simply bending over in the field, doing nothing.

"Mama!" I called from the path. Mother was apparently pretending she couldn't hear. I called her again and again. My voice soon disappeared into the hills and trees in the valley, and I felt empty. I suspected that she probably had wanted me to stay at the stream in the village. But I thought, "She taught me how to catch crabs; why wouldn't she want to speak to me here in the rice field?"

I felt sad and lonely. A moment passed before I realized she might be contemplating something. She was squatting, not moving at all. Yes, she must have been thinking.

"Mama!" I kept calling, but Mother kept ignoring me. I gradually lowered my voice. Finally I stopped calling her altogether.

She stayed in the rice field all day. By the time the sun set, she had worked her way to a distant spot in the field. She looked so small from where I stood, just the size of a small bean. As the sun set over the surrounding hills, the terraced fields grew dimmer, but the light lingered on the dry fields down by the large river. Someone was still working there with a bull, and both were bathed in the blazing red of the setting sun. I stood on the path for a long time and watched Mother. She looked like little more than a dark dot in the field.

Many years later, when I told my younger brother that Mother had taught me to catch crabs, he gave me a suspicious look. In fact, he seemed almost angry.

"That's impossible. Ma never liked to eat living creatures. No way she'd ever catch 'em."

I wanted to say, "You were asleep on her back, so of course you don't know what you're talking about. You didn't see her showing me the crabs at the *kawato*." Still, I held back.

As this was going through my mind, my brother added, "Ma'd never even kill a worm. When she bought a grilled mackerel from Miss O-tomi, she'd pull the flesh off the bone with her hands and distribute it on our plates, but she never ate any herself."

That was true. That memory stirred up others from my early youth. Miss O-tomi was the woman who sold seafood out of a large bamboo basket on her back. She would stop by our verandah with piles of grilled mackerel in her basket. She would save a large one for us because there were so many children in our family. Mother bought from her frequently and paid her at the end of each season. The grilled mackerel had a bamboo skewer pierced all the way from its tail to the mouth. It made the fish look reproachful even to us children, like it was twisting in the pattern of a wave and spitting the stick out of its mouth. Mother would hold the end of the skewer and flake away the flesh, giving each of us children an equal portion. After that, she might nibble a bit of flesh from the skewer but would not put any on her plate.

Despite my brother's protestations, I am certain I am not misremembering the scene of Mother holding the lantern over the stream on the way to take a bath. My guess is that she came to dislike meat and fish only toward the end of her life—maybe in her fifties, when I was not living close to her. When she was young (or at least before I was nine), she was full of life, in the very prime of womanhood. I cannot make sense of the vivid images I have of her plump, white calves, nor of the scene in which she stood in the water with her underwear peeking through the slit on the side of her work pants, but I went on listening to my brother's remembrances of Mother.

"We were always so poor, and Pa was so controlling that Ma couldn't express herself. Her credo was to be obedient and keep her head down. She was *too* obedient. Pa was the one who taught us to catch crabs, birds, rabbits, and other things. Ma really hated to touch living creatures. Instead, she preferred to go into the mountains and pick chestnuts, sweet acorns, and *matsutake* mushrooms."

Of course, I remember going to the mountains with her to pick seasonal nuts, fruits, and berries. I agree she was very good at picking them and could collect a lot in a short amount of time. She remembered precisely where the fruit trees were, and she clambered up the steep slope very quickly, saying she had to get there before others to get a good harvest. Nevertheless, I am plagued by the memory of that one evening when Mother went down to the stream, held the lantern over the water, and showed me the two entangled crabs. I remember how the dam stopped the flow of the water at the *kawato*, creating a gentle eddy. I remember how Mother circled the lantern over the water, which looked like clear, lightly colored glass. I remember how the two strange-looking crabs sat on the rock, legs entwined. Looking away from them and shifting my eyes to the foundation stone, I saw Mother's white ankles in the dark.

I wanted to say, "None of you knows a thing about Ma before she turned thirty." But I kept silent, fearing that if

I spoke, the image of Mother housed deep within me might somehow disintegrate.

The rice fields in the valley at dusk were aubergine in color, but the water in the rice paddies was reddish with the reflection of the sun setting in the west. Sloshing through the water, Mother walked between the green rice plants up to the ridge separating the paddies. Then she took off her work pants, strode over the *mito* water gate where the worms were, and went into the stream. It looked like she was washing her legs and groin. Before long she took off her upper kimono too. She scooped up some water and poured it over her shoulders and belly. I gazed at her from the foot of the mountain. After looking around cautiously, Mother stood up and stretched her back. She quickly put on the change of clothes she had carried up there in a basket on her back.

"Mama!" I ran the path up to the bank of the stream, and I sprung at her. I smelled the sweet and sour odor wafting from Mother's arms. Her body was cold.

As I clung to her, Mother asked repeatedly, "Were you up here in the hills? Were you up here playing the whole time?"

I felt terribly lonely. Rather than answer, I just cried, clinging to her tightly.

Translated by Kyoko Omori

Yumiura

Kawabata Yasunari

HIS DAUGHTER, TAGI, came to tell him that there was a woman at the door who said she'd met him thirty years earlier in Yumiura, Kyūshū. Kōzumi Shōzuke thought for a moment and decided that he might as well have the woman shown into the drawing room.

Unexpected callers came almost every day to see Kōzumi Shōzuke, the novelist—even now there were three guests in the drawing room. The three guests had come separately, but they were all talking together. It was about two o'clock on an afternoon unusually warm for the beginning of December.

Early in his career, KAWABATA YASUNARI (1899–1972) joined a group of experimental, modernist writers who identified themselves as the *Shin-kankaku-ha* (Neo-Perceptionist School). Ironically, however, Kawabata later earned a reputation as a quintessentially Japanese author because much of his later work describes the world of traditional Japanese aesthetics. In 1961 he won the Medal of Culture (the highest award bestowed by the Japanese government on artistic and literary figures), and in 1968 he became the first Japanese writer to win the Nobel Prize for Literature.

The fourth caller, the woman, knelt in the hall just outside the door she had opened, evidently embarrassed before the other guests.

"Please, come right in," Kōzumi said.

"Oh—it's truly, it's truly . . ." said the woman, in a voice that almost shook. "It's been such a long time! My name is Murano now, but when we met my name was Tai. Perhaps you remember?"

Kōzumi looked at the woman's face. She was a little past fifty, but she looked younger than her age—her pale cheeks were tinged with red. Her eyes were still large, despite her age. No doubt this was because she hadn't grown plump in middle age, as people often do.

"Just as I thought—you are the man I met. There's no doubt about it." The woman's eyes gleamed with pleasure as she stared at Kōzumi. There was an enthusiasm in her gaze that was lacking in Kōzumi's own as he looked back at her, trying to remember who she was. "You really haven't changed at all, have you? The line from your ear to your jaw, yes, and there—the area around your eyebrows—it's all just as it was. . . ." She pointed out each of his features, one by one, as if she were reciting a description of someone missing or wanted. Kōzumi felt embarrassed and also slightly worried at his own lack of memory.

The woman wore a black *haori* with her family crest embroidered on it in places, and with this an unostentatious kimono and obi. Her clothes were all well worn, but not enough to suggest that her family had fallen on hard times. Her body was small, as was her face. She wore no rings on her short fingers.

"Thirty years ago you came to the town of Yumiura—

or perhaps you've forgotten? You were kind enough to come by my room. It was the day of the Harbor Festival, toward evening. . . ."

"Hmm . . ."

Hearing that he had gone to the young woman's room—there was no doubt that she had been beautiful—Kōzumi tried once more to remember her. Thirty years ago Kōzumi had been twenty-four or twenty-five, and not yet married.

"You were with Kida Hiroshi and Akiyama Hisarō. The three of you had stopped at Nagasaki—you were traveling in Kyūshū. We invited you to attend a celebration that was being held in honor of the founding of a small newspaper in Yumiura."

Kida Hiroshi and Akiyama Hisarō were both dead, but in life they had been novelists some ten years Kōzumi's senior—writers who had befriended and encouraged him from the time he was twenty-two or twenty-three. Thirty years ago they had been novelists of the first rank. It was true that the two of them had spent some time in Nagasaki around then—Kōzumi remembered their diaries of those travels and anecdotes they had told about them, diaries and anecdotes that were certainly known to the literary public.

Kōzumi wasn't sure that he had been invited to go along on that trip to Nagasaki—he had just been starting out in the world—but as he searched his memories of Kida and Akiyama, those two role models of his, men who had influenced him so much, their faces rose up again and again before him—he remembered the numerous favors they had done him—he was drawn into a fond and tender mood of recollection. The expression on his face must have changed, for the woman spoke.

"You've remembered, haven't you?" she said. Her voice had changed, too. "I had just had my hair cut very short and I told you how embarrassed I was—how I felt cold from my ears to the back of my neck. Autumn was just about over, so it must have. . . . That newspaper had just been established in town, and I had gathered my courage and had my hair cut short so I could be a reporter—every time your eyes moved to my neck I'd turn as though I had been stung, to hide it from you. Oh, I remember it all so well! You came back to my room with me, and right away I opened my ribbon box and showed you the ribbons in it. I think I must have wanted to give you evidence—to prove that my hair had been long, that I had tied it up with ribbons until two or three days before. You were surprised at how many there were, but as a matter of fact I had always liked ribbons, ever since I was small."

The three other visitors remained silent. They had all discussed with Kōzumi the things they had come to discuss, but since there were other guests they had been sitting at ease, talking of this and that, when the woman arrived. It was only proper that they should pass Kōzumi on to this next visitor, allow him to speak with her—but there was also something in her manner that compelled them to be silent. Indeed, all three of the visitors avoided looking at the woman's face, or at Kōzumi's, and though they were able to hear what was being said, they tried not to look as if they were listening directly.

"When the newspaper company's celebration was over we went down a street in town, straight toward the ocean.

There was a sunset that seemed it might burst into flame at any moment. I'll never forget what you said then—that even the tiles on the roofs looked crimson, that even the back of my neck looked crimson. I replied that Yumiura was famous for its sunsets, and it was true—even now I can't forget them. That was the day we met—that day, with its beautiful sunset. The harbor was small, shaped like a bow—it looked like it had been carved out of the coast, there just under the mountains—and that's why it was named Yumiura, the bow-inlet. The colors of the sunset all collect there, in that scooped-out place. The high, rippled clouds in the sky at sunset that day seemed to be closer to the ground than the clouds one sees elsewhere, and the horizon out on the ocean seemed strangely close—it looked like the flocks of black birds that were migrating wouldn't have enough room to make it to the other side of the clouds. The colors of the sky didn't really seem to be reflected in the ocean, it seemed like that crimson had poured down only into the small ocean of the harbor and nowhere else. There was a festival boat decorated with flags on which people were beating drums and playing flutes, and there was a child on the boat—and you said that if you lit a match near that child's red kimono the whole ocean and the sky would burst instantly into flame, with a whoosh. Do you remember?"

"Yes, I think maybe I do. . . ."

"Since my husband and I married, my memory for things has gotten so bad it's pathetic. I guess there's no such thing as being so happy that you can decide not to forget. I know that people as happy and as busy as yourself don't have the time to sit around thinking of dull days from the past, and of course you really don't need to. . . . But Yumiura was the nicest town I've ever been in—in my whole life."

"Did you spend much time in Yumiura?" Kōzumi asked.

"Oh no—I got married and went to Numazu just six months after I met you there. Our older child has graduated from college and he's working now, and the younger, our daughter—she's old enough that we're hoping to find her a husband. I was born in Shizuoka, but because I didn't get along with my stepmother I was sent to live with relatives in Yumiura. I was eager to find some way to rebel, and so as soon as I arrived I went to work for the newspaper. I was called back and married off when my parents found out, so I was only in Yumiura for about seven months."

"And your husband is . . ."

"He's a priest at a Shintō shrine in Numazu."

This was not the sort of profession Kōzumi had been expecting, so he glanced up at the woman's face. The words "Fuji cut" are outdated and may end up giving the reader an unfavorable impression of the woman's hairstyle, but her hair was arranged in a pretty way with her bangs trimmed to resemble the slope of Mount Fuji. Kōzumi's eyes were drawn to it.

"We used to be able to live fairly well considering that he's a priest, but after the war things got tougher and tougher day by day until now—my son and daughter still stand by me, but they find all sorts of ways to defy their father."

Kōzumi sensed the disharmony of the woman's family.

"The shrine at Numazu is so big it doesn't even bear comparison with the shrine at that festival in Yumiura—

and of course the bigger they are the harder it is to manage them. We're having some problems just now because my husband decided to sell ten cedar trees that grew behind the temple without consulting anyone. I've run away—come here to Tōkyō."

"..."

"Memories are something we should be grateful for, don't you think? No matter what circumstances people end up in they're still able to remember things from the past— I think it must be a blessing bestowed on us by the gods. There were lots of children at the shrine on the road going through the town in Yumiura, so you suggested that we just keep going without stopping in—but even so we could see there were two or three flowers blooming on the small camellia over by the toilet—flowers with what they call 'double petals.' I still remember that camellia sometimes, even now—and I think what a wonderfully gentle person whoever planted it must have been."

It was clear that Kōzumi appeared as a character in one of the scenes in the woman's recollections of Yumiura. Images of that camellia and that bow-shaped harbor rose up in Kōzumi's mind as well now, seemingly called up by what the woman said. But it irritated him that he could not cross over into that country in the world of recollection where the woman lived. The two of them were as isolated from one another as the living and the dead of that country. Kōzumi's memory was weaker than that of most people his age. He sometimes talked at length with people whose faces he knew, yet could not remember their names—in fact it happened all the time. The unease he felt at such times was mixed with fear. And as he tried unsuccessfully to call up his own memories of the woman, his head began to ache.

"When I think about the person who planted that camellia, it seems, to me that I ought to have made my room there in Yumiura a little nicer. But I hadn't and so you only came that once, and then thirty years passed without us ever meeting. Though to tell the truth I'd decorated my room a little even then, to make it look more like a young woman's."

Kōzumi could remember nothing at all of her room. Perhaps wrinkles formed on his forehead, perhaps his expression became slightly severe, for the woman's next words showed that she was preparing to leave.

"I must apologize for having come so suddenly, that was rude. . . . But I've wanted to see you for such a long time, and coming here has really been such a pleasure for me—nothing would have made me happier. I wonder—would you mind very much if I came again sometime?—if I could—there are some things I'd like to discuss."

"That would be fine."

The woman's tone voice suggested that there was something she was not saying, something she hesitated to say in front of the other guests. And when Kōzumi walked out into the hall to see her off, the instant he slid the door shut behind him, the woman let her stiff body slacken. Kōzumi could hardly believe his eyes. This was the way a woman held her body when she was with a man she had slept with.

"Was that your daughter earlier?"

"Yes."

"I'm afraid I didn't see your wife. . . ."

Kōzumi walked out into the entryway ahead of the

woman without answering. He addressed her back as she bent down to put on her sandals in the entryway.

"So I went all the way to your room, in a town called Yumiura."

"Yes." The woman looked back over her shoulder. "You asked me to marry you. In my room."

"What?"

"I was already engaged to my husband at the time—I told you that, and refused, but . . ."

It was as though Kōzumi's heart had been pierced with a pin. No matter how bad his memory had gotten, to think that he should entirely forget having proposed marriage to a young woman—to be almost unable to remember that young woman—he didn't even feel surprised, no—it struck him as grotesque. He had never been the sort of young man to propose marriage lightly.

"You were kind enough to understand the circumstances that made it necessary for me to refuse," the woman said, her large eyes filling with tears. Then, her short fingers trembling, she took a photograph from her purse. "These are my children. My daughter is much taller than I was, but she looks very much like I did when I was young."

The young woman was small in the photograph, but her eyes sparkled brightly and she had a beautiful face. Kōzumi stared at the picture, attempting to make himself remember having met a young woman like this some thirty years earlier on a trip and having asked her to marry him.

"I'll bring my daughter sometime, if you don't mind— then if you like you can see how I used to be." It sounded as though there were tears mixed in with the woman's voice. "I've told my son and daughter everything, so they know all about you. They speak of you as though you were an old friend. I had really terrible morning sickness both times, sometimes I got a little crazy—but then as the morning sickness started getting better, around the time when the child started moving—it's odd but somehow I'd start wondering if the child might not be yours. Sometimes in the kitchen I'd sharpen a knife. . . . I've told my children about all that, too."

"You . . . don't ever do that."

Kōzumi was unable to continue.

At any rate, it appeared that the woman had suffered extremely because of Kōzumi. Even her family had. . . . Or perhaps on the other hand a life of extreme suffering had been made easier for her by virtue of her memories of Kōzumi. Even her family had been affected. . . .

But that past—her unexpected meeting with Kōzumi in the town called Yumiura—had evidently gone on living strongly inside the woman, while in Kōzumi, who had committed a sort of sin, it had been extinguished, utterly lost.

"Shall I leave the picture with you?" she asked, to which Kōzumi replied by shaking his head. "No, don't."

The small woman walked with short steps through the gate and then vanished beyond it.

Kōzumi took a detailed map of Japan and a book in which the names of all the cities, towns, and villages in the country were listed down from a bookshelf and brought it back into the sitting room. He had the three visitors search with him, but neither he nor any of them was able to find a town by the name of Yumiura anywhere in Kyūshū.

"It's very strange," Kōzumi said, looking up. Then he

closed his eyes and thought. "I don't remember ever having gone to Kyūshū before the war. No, I'm sure I didn't
go. That's right—I was sent on an airplane to a base the
Special Attack Forces had in Shikaya during the battle in
Okinawa—I went as a reporter for the navy—that was the
first time I went to Kyūshū. The next time was when I went
to see Nagasaki just after the atom bomb was dropped.
That was when I heard the stories about Mr. Kida and Mr.
Akiyama—about their having gone there thirty years earlier, from people in Nagasaki."

The three guests put forward a number of opinions
about the woman's fantasies or delusions, laughing all the
while. The conclusion was, of course, that the woman was
crazy. But Kōzumi couldn't help thinking that he was crazy,
too. He had sat listening to the woman's story, half believing and half doubting that what she said was true, searching his memory. It happened that in this case there wasn't
even a town called Yumiura, but who could say how much
of Kōzumi's past others remembered, though Kōzumi had
forgotten it himself—though it no longer existed within
him. The woman who had come that day would almost
certainly go on believing even after Kōzumi died that he
had proposed to her in Yumiura. Either way it was the
same.

Translated by Michael Emmerich

The Snow of Memory

Takahashi Mutsuo

I HAVE A PHOTOGRAPH.

This photo, which has browned with age, is taller than it is wide and has roughly the same proportions as a playing card. In it stands my mother. She is leaning upon a waist-high set of shelves against the wall of what appears to be the interior of a photography studio. She is wearing a coat of iridescent *tamamushi* material over an under-kimono decorated with a striped pattern, and her hair is up in the rounded hairdo traditionally worn by married women. On her right is a little boy with his hair cropped

---

TAKAHASHI MUTSUO (1937–) is one of Japan's most prominent living poets, with over two dozen anthologies of poetry and numerous literary prizes to his name. Though most active in the realm of free verse, he has frequently crossed the barriers of literary genre and written traditional Japanese poetry, novels, Nō and Kyōgen plays, reworkings of ancient Greek dramas and epic poetry, countless works of literary criticism, and even an opera libretto. This selection comes from the first essay in his 1970 memoir, *Jū-ni no enkei* (Twelve Perspectives), about the time he spent as an impoverished, fatherless boy in the southern island of Kyūshū.

close. That is me as a boy, probably three years old. I am seated on top of the shelves with my back against the wall, and I am wearing a white turtleneck sweater under a three-piece suit that looks too grown-up for my age.

Here and there, little flecks of black and white are visible against the background of the suit. You can see them on my jacket, vest, and pants. These little flecks of black and white look like snow. The white flecks remind me of snowflakes falling from the sky to the earth below, and the black flecks look like dull flecks of snow that have fallen to the ground and become soiled. Beside me on top of the shelf is a black vase. Even though it is almost the same size as my head, it is positioned so that it looks as if I am holding it in my right hand. Inside are several branches of a plum tree covered with blossoms. Come to think of it, the petals of the plum blossoms also look like snowflakes floating in the air.

As I remember it, snow was falling that day. When I slid open the wooden doors of my grandmother's house and went outside in response to my mother's urging, the sky hung down heavily over us. At the same time, however, part of the cloudy sky seemed to be swollen with light, almost like the insides of a frothy, spoiled egg. Snow was gently falling from the spot where the heavens harbored the light inside, but when the flakes reached the dirty patch of earth in front of our house, they simply disappeared. Likewise, when they fell in the water beyond the embankment on the far side of our yard, they turned the color of the sky and vanished in the murky water.

We went along the road by the embankment, passing the houses of the Kawahara and Kaneko families, and then we turned. When we reached the main road, my playmate Kakko-chan from the Hashimoto family jumped out, pointed at my mother's rounded hairdo, and started jeering, "Bride! Look at the newlywed!" I seem to remember she was wearing black rayon work pants and a jacket with an apron over everything.

We climbed into the rickshaw waiting for us in front of the Hashimotos' house. First Mother got in, then I climbed onto her lap. Once we were situated, the rickshaw driver threw a worn-out fuzzy quilt over my lap. He lowered the hood of the rickshaw in front of us to shield us from the weather then started to pull the rickshaw forward.

In the center of the hood of the rickshaw was a celluloid window so that we could peek at the world outside. From where I was seated on my mother's lap, the window was directly in front of me, but it was too high to see much more than sky. The celluloid of the window had turned slightly yellow and taken on an irregular warp, perhaps from weathering the wind and rain. Through the yellow, warped window, I watched the yellow snow fall in a twisted trajectory toward the earth.

The rickshaw climbed up and down hills, crossed railroad tracks, and passed through house-lined streets. From Mother's lap, I felt the warmth of her body and, along with it, the quick movement of the rickshaw rolling forward. Each time the rickshaw rolled up an incline, down a slope, or across a flat stretch of ground, I sensed the change of direction through the jolts in her lap. Meanwhile, I watched the snow through the plastic window. As we moved, its downward path appeared to shift through the warped window. When the rickshaw stopped temporarily but did not change direction, I could tell we had come to a railroad crossing. As I watched the movement of the snow falling in its warped trajectory outside the window, I heard the gasp of a steam whistle from a boiler car that was stopped by the switch on the tracks. The sound of the whistle and the movement of the snow seemed to mingle with one another.

The photography studio was located on the edge of a red-light district in the coal-mining town of Naokata in northern Kyūshū. By the time we got there, it must have been late morning, probably about ten o'clock. The driver lowered the poles of the rickshaw so that we shifted forward and angled down somewhat. After he raised the hood, the driver embraced me, lifted me from where I sat unstably on Mother's knees, and set me on the ground. The door of the photography studio was a cracked glass door, splattered with mud. To hold the cracked glass in place, someone had pasted patches of the kind of Japanese paper ordinarily used on sliding doors. These patches were cut in the shape of cherry blossoms. Despite the mud and paper patches, the mirror-like surface of the glass reflected a deep, silent vision of the falling snow. The ground was speckled with black and white snowflakes.

Perhaps because of the snow, there were no other customers. We were probably the first ones that day. The photographer brought a brazier with hot coals so we could warm up. Still, the studio with its high ceilings, wooden walls, and spacious interior did not seem to grow any warmer. As I trembled in the cold, the photographer seated me on top of the shelves by the wall and positioned my mother beside me. He then lifted up the cloth at the back of his big box

camera—the cloth was black on the outside but lined with
red inside—and peered through the lens. The reason that I
look so bullnecked in the picture he took that day is because
of the cold in the dusty room. By the time the photographer
ushered us outside, there was a slight accumulation of snow,
which hid the ground from view.

Why do I remember these details so well after all these years?
I remember because my mother disappeared soon after the
day we went to the photographer's studio. Mother's disappearance probably superimposed itself over my memories of
the falling snow—a quite unusual event in Kyūshū—and
produced a clear image of the scene in the dark depths of my
unconscious mind.

I also remember with great clarity the day my mother
disappeared. It was one of those days in early spring when
the breeze still had a slight chill to it, when the wind had
grown so calm that it could easily lull you to sleep before
you even knew it. My mother was wearing her iridescent
tamamushi coat over her *yagasuri* under-kimono that day,
just like before. This time, she was also clutching to her
breast a little package wrapped in a folded, purple cloth.
Mother never wore makeup, but for some reason that day
she smelled of the sweet, dusty powder women sometimes
put on to whiten their faces. I remember thinking that was
the smell of someone who had put on their best clothes to
leave for someplace special.

"I'm going into town for a bit. Be good and wait for me
like a big boy."

As far as I remember, I only nodded. I don't think I said
anything at all. She began walking.

My grandmother's house, where we were living at the

time, was next to a little reservoir lined with an embankment. The road that went alongside it passed the earthen plot of land in front of Grandmother's house. Two doors down, the road disappeared behind some houses but then reappeared a little further down. For a little while it followed the embankment along a low hill, but as it curved around the far side of the hill, it once again vanished from view. From there it gradually descended between some steel factories, crossed some railroad tracks, and continued through town.

I stood there watching Mother. She disappeared for a moment behind the houses then reemerged on the other side, becoming part of the distant landscape. I watched until she disappeared for good, hidden by the bank of the hill. No, that's not entirely true. I continued to stand there even well after she had disappeared from sight. Mother did something unusual—she looked back over her shoulder, turned, and looked back over her shoulder again. Each time, she waved at me.

I don't think there was anyone else home when she left. I know it sounds strange that she left me all alone, but in my memories, at least, there wasn't anyone else around. When Grandmother returned home that evening, I asked her, "Grandma? Isn't Mommy back yet?"

"She'll be back soon."

But three days passed. Ten days passed. Still, Mother did not come home.

"Isn't she back yet?"

"Be a big boy. She'll be back in no time at all," Grandmother answered me as she turned the handle of her stone mill. A month later, Mother still had not come home.

Then after three months, a big package arrived for me

in the mail. It was from my mother. Inside, I found choco-late, hard candy, a toy paper parachute, and some picture books. That was when my grandmother finally told me the truth.

"Your mommy went to China."

I threw the paper parachute into the air, but it got stuck on a branch of the persimmon tree beside the storage shed. I had the strange feeling that my mother was not in some far, far away place called China, but that she simply was no longer anywhere at all. The rainy season was just drawing to a close.

When I think back on these memories, it was the day I looked at the snow through the window of the rickshaw that marks the crucial turning point when my mother started to disappear into the distance, leaving me all alone. In a sense, my earliest memories are on the far side of that snow. When I think back upon them, I do so through that snowy veil.

The snow of memory . . . It is not always white. Just as the snow falling that day looked yellow through the cellu-loid window of the rickshaw, the snow of memory turns yellow and browns with age. For that reason, the pho-tographs of the deep snows of yesteryear that we retain in our minds are also yellowed and brown.

The snow of memory does not necessary fall down in a straight line. Like the falling snow that seemed to warp in midair as I watched it through the celluloid window, the snow of memory often falls in a warped path. Indeed, the images of long ago that we retain in our memories are just as warped.

The warping of memory also arises from the fact that memory and hearsay tend to intermingle. Before we know it, we can no longer distinguish which is which. In my case, all of my memories before my third birthday are that way. For instance, I can remember my mother putting me on her back when I was two and walking down the stone staircase behind my grandmother's house, but I am not sure if that is my own memory, free of outside interference, or if my grandmother told me about that and the image she helped construct simply took on the form of a memory. Perhaps both are true; hearsay and memory have supplemented one another to form a single image in my mind. I am not sure.

A year passed after my mother's disappearance.

One morning a young relative of mine whom we had nicknamed Non-chan came to the house. She was dressed in her best clothes, much like my mother was that day when we went to have the photograph taken. She definitely had the air of someone dressed up to go somewhere special. I had associated going away with countless little flecks of black and white snow, but that day there was no snow falling. It was as warm as the day Mother disappeared. About a foot over Non-chan's head, two yellow butterflies flitted around one another in midair.

Non-chan took my hand and led me into a train. She had not said anything to me, but I clearly understood we were about to go to meet Mother who had disappeared so many months before. Non-chan sat with her back to the front of the train, while I sat across from her, quietly looking out the window.

We took the Chikuhō Line from Naokata, transferred to the Kagoshima Main Line at Orio, and took the newly completed underwater Kanmon tunnel connecting the northern tip of Kyūshū to the city of Shimonoseki on Honshū. By the time we arrived in Shimonoseki, it was probably past two in the afternoon. The newly built station was still heated with steam, giving it a wintry smell that evoked nostalgic memories. As we passed in front of the station dining room, I smelled a thick omelet frying in a skillet.

Shimonoseki is a long, narrow port town with many slopes that all descend to the sea. As we rushed from the new station to the hotel where I was sure we would find my mother, we took a flat road that crossed many of these sloping streets. Each time there was a break in the clusters of warehouses and other buildings lining the streets, I caught a glimpse of the sea, which was an unusually deep blue.

We found ourselves in a flagstone-covered square near the pier where the ferry from Korea arrives in Shimonoseki. The square was surrounded on three sides by buildings, and on the one that faced the sea, there was a hotel named Fujikichi. We went inside. A woman wearing a white cook's apron quickly led us to the third floor. She said something to another woman by a bay window. The other woman had been holding up a newspaper that hid her face, but when she heard the woman from the hotel speaking to her, she folded the newspaper and looked our way.

The light of noon flooded through the window so that the seated woman seemed to float in back lighting. She was wrapped in cloak of light, as if she were some mystery woman from far, far away. She looked at me and smiled.

"My little Mut-chan."

The lady crossing her legs in the wicker chair was my mother. Reflections from the sea far below filled the room with tiny droplets of light (droplets, not little flakes of snow). The shimmering light danced over her calves.

She was wearing a pale aqua, sleeveless Chinese-style dress decorated with a small navy-blue clover pattern. She was smoking a cigarette, and on the ring finger of the hand holding it was a deep green piece of jade. As my gaze traveled from the finger sporting the jade ring to the palm of her hand and her forearms, her skin seemed to grow ever paler. I could not help noticing that the blood vessels, which were of a lighter green than the jade, seemed to press up against her skin.

Perhaps these subtle changes were from the cold climate of northern China where Mother had been for the last year. The cold there penetrates to the bone, even when you wear three pairs of woolen socks on top of one another. Or perhaps these changes were due to the shady days she had spent there—days full of things at which others could not even guess. Whichever it was, during her time in China, she must have experienced snowfalls so deep and heavy they would dwarf any she had seen in northern Kyūshū.

After leaving me, Mother had gone across the Korea Strait, through Korea, and across the Yalu River into China. Her destination was the mansion of a Japanese gentleman by the name of Ōkushi Kanjirō who lived in Tianjin. Mr. Ōkushi was from Saga in northwest Kyūshū, but he had gone to China at a young age. Once there, he began doing an extensive business in buttons and other decorative accoutrements. In the process, he amassed what

appears to have been quite a fortune. It was when he was
in his fifties that Mr. Ōkushi met my mother, who was
temporarily working as a parlor maid in a Japanese-style
inn in Shimonoseki.

Based on the stories Mother told me later, I can call up
a thorough image of the house where they lived in the
Japanese concessions of Tianjin. The house was an unnec-
essarily spacious Japanese-style building in what was more
or less a malformed square. From the front, it appeared to
be a one-story house with unusually high eaves, but the
inside was roomy, with as many as three stories. Outside,
about where the second story would be, there hung a large
sign with gilt lettering that read ŌKUSHI KANJIRŌ BUTTON
SHOP, spelled out from right to left in a horizontal row of
Chinese characters. The front part of the ground floor was
a shop with buttons lined up all in rows, while the back part
served as offices. The Ōkushi family and their servants
lived on the upper floors.

Mother served both as Mr. Ōkushi's secretary and as his
children's nanny, and so she was given a cheerless room on
the third floor as her living quarters. All of the rooms on
that floor had originally been used to warehouse merchan-
dise and other things, but one of the rooms had been
cleared out for the newly arrived resident. There was one
window, and beneath that only a desk, a chair, and a bed.
Even so, I imagine my mother filled the room with a feminine, flamboyant flair in no time at all.

Making the excuse that he wanted to make rounds of
the storage rooms, Mr. Ōkushi often came to the third
floor in the middle of the night. My mother had to take
great pains to greet her lover silently, without raising any

noise. The private rooms of Mr. Ōkushi and his wife were directly below Mother's.

Breakfast was served in the dining room on the second floor, and the entire family ate there, including the servants. Mr. Ōkushi sat in the seat of honor at the rectangular table while his wife and my mother sat on opposite. Right next to him were his second and third sons, but the eldest son sat next to Mother. Finally, the other servants sat in a row off to the right and left. This line-up was frequently put in disarray by the fact that the second and third sons wanted to come to sit by my mother's side. All three of the Ōkushi boys were far fonder of my mother than their own.

Mrs. Ōkushi always treated Mother, who sat opposite her at the table, like an older sister might treat a far younger sister. Still, who was there to know their real feelings? Sometimes when Mr. Ōkushi had some business that kept him away from the breakfast table, his wife would scold her sons when they wanted to sit by my mother. The two women would sit with silence reigning between.

At some point during her stay in China, Mother apparently became pregnant with Mr. Ōkushi's child and snuck off to a doctor in the French concession for an abortion. Mother hated even the slightest evidence of sexuality. As if that were not enough to keep her quiet, this was during the war, when abortion was still considered a form of homicide. Her relationship with Mr. Ōkushi and the abortion were topics that should have been strictly off limits, but somehow, I managed to find out about her transgressions. Perhaps when I saw her fair-skinned hand with that large jade ring and pronounced veins, I vaguely sensed all

that had befallen her that year, although I had not wit-
nessed any of it directly.

The abortion probably took place soon after her arrival
at the Ōkushi household. If so, it would have been toward
the beginning of spring when the final snowflakes of the
season were falling upon the pavement and melting, falling
and melting over and over again. It is not impossible that
Mother's entire trip to China was in order to abort the
unwanted product of their liaison in Shimonoseki.

This is how I imagine the scene. The apartment of the
outlaw doctor, who lives in a state of self-imposed exile
from the outside world, is on the third or fourth floor of a
six-story building. My mother is lying on a simple bed
next to the wall, opening her eyes, which are bleary from
exhaustion after the procedure. On the opposite wall is a
double window that opens outward, and below that is a
simple triangular cupboard on which the doctor has laid his
surgical tools. A square metal basin sits on top of the cupboard. Inside, a bloody fetus takes its final shallow breaths.

Mother sees this. Behind the bloody fetus, black velvet
curtains hang from the ceiling, covering most of the double window. They are mostly drawn, but there is a slight
gap between them. Outside, she can see snow falling.
Because of the double panes of glass meant to keep out the
cold, the snow looks warped, just as it did through the celluloid window in the hood of the rickshaw that day we
went to the photography studio. Steam is rising from the
stove in the corner of the room.

The bloody fetus at which Mother gazes is not just a
newly aborted child. It is me. She had decided to be a wo-

man rather than a mother, and as proof of this choice, she had sacrificed her fetus. She had sacrificed my blood. . . .

"Look! It's your mom, go on!"

When Non-chan said this, I began edging nervously backward, away from the window that looked out over the sea and that spilled the reflection of the silvery waves into the room. My eyes were still fixed upon Mother.

"What a funny boy! Are you shy?"

Non-chan looked at my mother and smiled. Neither Non-chan nor Mother was aware of it, but during the year of her absence, Mother had become someone other than herself, someone who was a complete stranger to me.

After that, Mother came to live with us in my grandmother's house. When I entered grade school at the publicly funded Citizen's School, we moved to be near my school in Kamenko, and together we stayed in the house of an old lady everyone called "the single granny," who made her living selling cheap candy. For a good while the task before me was to try to figure out how to restore the old image of my mother and me that remained in my memory from before her disappearance. I had to figure out how to apply that image to this woman who had, for the time being, become a stranger I did not recognize.

Still, despite my efforts, the mother within me, the mother from my past who resides on the far side of the yellowed snow of memory, never returned again.

Translated by Jeffrey Angles

Bones

Shima Tsuyoshi

THE WORK CREW had arrived at the construction site and was taking a break when a yellow safety helmet swung into view at the foot of the hill. The man in the helmet was moving at a fast clip as he made his way up the dirt road that cut through the pampas grass. Right behind him was an old woman. She relied on a walking stick, but she dogged the man like a shadow.

The construction site was situated atop a stretch of foothills from which one could see the entire city of Naha in a single sweep. Long, long ago the area had been cov-

---

SHIMA TSUYOSHI (1939–) made a name for himself as a writer while working as civil servant in the Office of Education of the Okinawan Prefectural government. Although his writing spans several genres, including fiction, drama, film scenarios, and historical nonfiction, much of his work has been about Okinawa and the dramatic changes it has undergone, especially during the traumatic years of World War II. This story appeared in *Ryūkyū shinpō* (Ryūkyū News) in 1973, a year after Okinawa reverted to Japanese control after nearly thirty years of American occupation. The reversion brought a great deal of investment from the Japanese mainland, but as this story suggests, the economic development that ensued sometimes turned up old and bitter memories.

ered in trees, and many a tale had been told about the ghosts who resided in the dark, densely wooded hills. But that was until the war. The heavy naval bombardment from offshore had leveled the *akagi* forests down to the last tree. And then came the postwar expansion of the city that had altered the way the land looked down below once and for all. It was as though the whole area had been painted over in colors that gave it a bright, gaudy look. The denuded slope was like a half-peeled papaya. The top had been lopped off, and from there to the road a quarter of the way down the hill the red clay was exposed to the elements. According to the notice posted at the construction site, the hilltop was slated to become the site of a twenty-story luxury hotel.

The five men in the work crew were from Naha City Hall. Sitting under the shade of a giant banyan tree, they gazed at the city as it stretched before them. The plain was flat and dry and looked as though it had been lightly dusted in a silvery powder. The August sun had risen to a point in the sky where it was now almost directly overhead. As the light danced over the whitecaps that broke against the coral reef lying offshore, it seemed almost playful. It was as though the sun had come to make fun of the men and the bored, fed-up expressions they wore on their faces. Meanwhile, some forty to fifty feet from the tree sat a big bulldozer. It was resting quietly for the moment, but the prongs on the shovel were pointed toward the workers. It was just about there, too—the spot where the bulldozer was parked—that the bones had turned up the day before.

The man in the yellow safety helmet nodded in the direction of the assistant section chief as he approached the work crew from city hall. He was the man in charge of the construction site, and the company name, Toa Electric, was embroidered on his breast pocket in fancy gold letters. They glittered in the sunlight.

"Well, where are the bones?" asked the assistant section chief, a round-shouldered man. He had grabbed a shovel and looked as though he was ready to get to work right away.

"I hate to say it, but there's been a new hitch." As the construction boss turned and looked behind him, the metal rims of his glasses seemed to flash as they caught the light of the sun.

There was the old woman—her neck thrust forward, her withered chin jutting out prominently into the air. She was out of breath from keeping up with the man in the yellow safety hat as they had climbed the long incline.

"So where is it, this spot you're talking about?"

There was a razor-sharp edge to the man's voice as he turned to address the old woman. With that, she lifted her walking stick and pointed it at the men from city hall.

"That's it there. I'm sure of it. Because the tree marks the spot. Any place from the tree to where you've got your bulldozer parked over there is where you'll find 'em. Yes sir, underneath it's nothing but bones. I know 'cause I saw it all with my own two eyes. There's no mistake. I'm absolutely certain of it."

The construction boss could hardly believe what he was being told and turned to the assistant section chief with a look of total incredulity.

"I never thought I'd have a mess like this on my hands. It wasn't until this morning that these people let me know there was a *graveyard* up here."

The construction boss introduced the old woman to the assistant section chief. She was the former owner of the property, and her family name was Higa. Higa Kame. Her given name sounded the same as the word for turtle, and the boss could not help feeling there was something tortoise-like about the old woman's appearance.

The turtle woman cut him short. "No, Mister, this is no graveyard. We just dug a hole and threw the bodies in. That's all there was to it. We were in the middle of a war here on the island, and nothing more could be done."

"But that's exactly what I needed to hear from you. Why in hell didn't you say something about graves before now? Letting heavy-duty equipment sit idle even for one day costs a fortune. We're taking a big loss."

The anger in the man's voice was countered by an equally furious look from the old turtle woman. Her aging, yellowed eyes had peaked into small triangles, and her lips were tightly pursed. The assistant section chief tossed his shovel aside. He knew trouble and could see it coming now.

"What kind of numbers are we talking about here?" he asked uneasily.

"Thousands. The mayor had us gather up all the bodies from around here and put them in a pile. There were so many you couldn't begin to count 'em. . . ." The old woman waved her stick in the air as if to make her point. Doubt-less she was having trouble expressing herself in standard Japanese and felt the need to emphasize what she had to say.

"That many, huh?" A look of despair crossed the assis-tant section chief's face.

"There were so many bodies they wouldn't fit in the hole. Later on we used gasoline to burn them and then buried the ashes. The mayor said he'd look after the up-keep of the site, but then we never heard another word from him. Pour souls. There was no one to care for them when they died, and now their bones have been completely abandoned."

"That's not how I heard it. No sirree, that's not the story I was told." The frustration and anger in the construction boss's voice was almost palpable as he spat out the words in his own local Ōsaka dialect from mainland Japan.

No, that was not the story.

It was a line from the script recited to him by the people down at city hall. But the line was supposed to be delivered by them to him, not by him to someone else.

It was yesterday when he had phoned them from the construction site to say unmarked graves had been uncovered on the hill and that the company was asking city hall to step in and deal with the problem.

"Unmarked graves are the responsibility of the Health and Physical Education Section," he was told. "They're the ones to handle it."

But then again, if he was talking about the bones of war dead, "Well, *no, that was a another story altogether.*"

"Where's a phone around here?" The assistant section chief seemed to have decided on some plan of action and needed to report it to the office.

The boss took the lead as the two men headed up the red clay slope of the hill. The others remained seated on the ground, watching the boss and the assistant section chief disappear into the distance.

The first to speak was the oldest member in the group. He was wearing a pair of rubber work boots. "Ma'am, when you say 'bones,' are you talking about the bones of mainland Japanese?"

The turtle woman inched her way under the big banyan tree. Her lips were in constant motion. It was as if she were chewing on something or muttering to herself. "Hell, what does it matter whose bones they are? They all died in the big battle. Japanese. Americans. Men. Women. Even little babies got killed while they were still sucking at their mothers' breasts. We dumped them all together into this one big pit."

"You mean there really are thousands of bodies buried under here?" This time it was the fellow with only one eye who spoke. He could hardly believe what the old woman had said.

"They talked about putting up a memorial stone. That's what the mayor told us, and that's why my father planted this tree to mark the spot."

Without thinking, the men let their eyes scan the tree that branched overhead. Now that she had mentioned it, there *was* something strange about a banyan tree growing here. But there it was, standing in the middle of a field of pampas grass. It had been free to grow as it pleased, and, tropical plant that it was, it had shot up to a height of ten yards. From its boughs hung a long red beard of tendrils that reached all the way to the ground.

"That means it's twenty-eight years old." The one-eyed jack blew a puff of smoke from his lips. He sounded impressed at the thought of how much the tree had grown.

"And, ma'am, that means when you got the boss here to

buy the land you pretended not to know about the bones, right?" This time it was the youngster in the group who spoke up. What with a crop of whiskers on his chin, he looked like a hippie, and there was a smart-alecky grin on his face.

"No, idiot. The reason the company got the property was . . ." The old woman sprayed the area with the spittle that flew from the gap between her missing two front teeth. "It was all because of that dumb son of ours. He let the real estate agent pull the wool over his eyes. We tried to educate him. We tried to get him to understand what sort of property it was and that it ought not to be sold, but he never got the point."

It was not long before the assistant section chief and the construction boss were back. They both looked agitated.

"We've got no choice. We're the ones who will have to step in and deal with the problem, and that's that. The government is ducking it at both the national and prefectural levels, saying there's no budget. Or any manpower. That means we're elected for the job. So let's get to work." The assistant section chief turned to his men and addressed them in a voice that was more mature than expected for a person his age.

But no one moved. The men continued to sit, smoking their cigarettes and wearing the same dull expressions that had been on their faces all morning. The construction company boss studied them with a forlorn, even helpless, look. "Just how many days is this going to take, anyway," he asked.

"Hmm, I wonder. After all, these are the only men we could muster from the city's Disinfection Unit. With such a small crew, there's no telling how long it might take," replied the assistant section chief.

The construction boss walked in a circle, trampling the thick clumps of summer grass underfoot. It appeared he had some sort of plan in mind. Suddenly he stopped in his tracks and looked up, turning the full force of his charming baby face on the crew. "First, I must ask you men not to let anyone from the newspapers get wind of what's happening here. Once the press gets to shouting about it, we'll have a real mess on our hands."

The assistant section chief had a questioning look in his eye as he closely studied the construction boss's face. He seemed to be stumped and not fully prepared to digest what the boss might say next.

"We don't want any news to get out that will damage the future image of the hotel."

The assistant section chief nodded in agreement. Clearly, something in the boss's argument had impressed and persuaded him.

But by then Hippie-Beard was already on his feet. "Here we go again. And whose ass are we wiping this time? I can't believe we are going to do this." His heavy, gong-like voice resonated in the air. Yet if he was being sarcastic, his remarks seemed aimed at no one in particular.

"It's a helluva lot better than having to dig up undetonated bombs," piped up One-Eyed Jack.

All the men from city hall knew what he was talking about. They also knew he had a history of dropping explosives overboard in the ocean to catch fish illegally, and this was how he had lost an eye.

"Anyway, we start work right after lunch," announced the assistant section chief.

But Kamakichi was in no hurry, and he was the last member of the crew to get to his feet. The shadow that the big banyan tree cast on the ground had shrunk to nothing by now. In the distance, the cicadas were droning away. The mere thought of what was about to unfold was enough to make Kamakichi depressed. And, try as he might, he could not help feeling this way.

It was a little past noon the following day when the first bones began to surface. The men had been digging all morning, and until then the only noticeable change had been in the color of the soil as it turned from red to gray. As they dug deeper, they began to find some white things that looked like pieces of broken clamshells scattered in the powdered soil. Perhaps they only imagined it, but the earth seemed to give off the odor of rotting flesh.

"It's like the old woman said. The upper layer is all ashes."

The assistant section chief directed his crew to spread a canvas tarp along the edge of the pit. Kamakichi and the man in the rubber work boots were put to work doing the sorting. When each spadeful of dirt and ash was shoveled out of the hole, their job was to pick out the pieces of bone and put them in a burlap bag. Because the small, cremated pieces of bone had been reduced almost to a powder, it was impossible to identify any of them as belonging to a particular part of the human anatomy. Kamakichi closed his eyes. It was with a sinking feeling of dread and disgust that he forced his hands to sift through the piles of ashes.

The work went at a livelier pace once whole pieces of bone began to emerge from the pit. The gloomier the job became, the more it seemed, paradoxically, to raise the men's spirits. From out of the ashes came two round objects about the size of ping-pong balls.

"What're these?" When Kamakichi showed them to the man in the boots, Rubber Boots laughed and thrust them in the direction of Kamakichi's crotch.

"Fossilized balls."

All at once the men roared with laughter.

"No, no. It's not right to laugh at the dead. They're all bodhisattvas now, you know." The assistant section chief looked very serious, befitting his position of responsibility, and there was a mildly admonishing tone in his voice. "That's the hinge ball where the femur attaches to the hip-bone."

"I bet you were born after the war," said Rubber Boots to Kamakichi.

Kamakichi felt as if the older man was trying to make fun of him. As for the war, he had no memory of it. "I was two when the war ended."

"Why, it's practically the same thing. If you ask me it seems like, ever since the war, we've all kept on living here in these islands by picking our way through a huge pile of bones. That's what's kept us going."

"Back then, nobody batted an eye at the thought of sleeping with a corpse," chimed in One-Eyed Jack.

Rubber Boots went on with what he was saying. He spoke with the authority of an older person who was the senior member of the work crew. "I was in the local defense forces when I was taken prisoner. One day I discovered a patch of big, white daikon growing in a field not far from the POW camp. But when I went to dig them out of the ground, I found they were growing on top of a huge mound of bones."

"Did you eat 'em?" asked Hippie-Beard.

"Of course I did. What do you think?"

Once again the men roared with laughter.

"It's the dead protecting the living," said One-Eyed Jack. The tone of his voice was almost reverential.

"This here banyan tree is a lot like us. It's had good fertilizer." Rubber Boots stretched himself upward from the waist and craned his neck to peer up at the tree.

"It's the same for everybody here in Okinawa," added One-Eyed Jack, sounding almost as if he were making excuses for himself.

"That may be true, but what about the others? You know, the ones who've used their fellow Okinawans as bonemeal to feed off and make themselves rich and fat." It was Hippie-Beard speaking up again. He had been born after the war but was determined not to let this conversation pass without putting in his two cents.

"So just who is it you're talking about?" One-Eyed Jack had turned serious.

But now Hippie-Beard got flustered, at a loss to explain.

As Kamakichi sorted out the pieces of bone, he could feel his gorge rising, and he had to swallow hard from time to time just to be able to keep working. He felt oddly out of place amid the lively banter of the other men in the work crew. What they were saying struck him as terribly disrespectful, even blasphemous, toward the dead. At the same time, he kept trying to tell himself that the bones were just objects, no different from what one might find in an archaeological dig of an old shell mound.

In the afternoon, as the men began to let their pace slacken, all at once the old woman silently reappeared, as if out of nowhere. They welcomed her back, trying to joke with her about the job they were doing. But she would have no part of it. She hunkered down next to Kamakichi and began to study the pile of bones. As always, her mouth was in constant but wordless motion.

"Hey, ma'am. Afterward we want you to do a good job of saying prayers for the dead buried here to rest in peace. Otherwise, there'll be hell to pay if so many lost souls get out and start wandering all over the place." The assistant section chief seemed to be in an uncharacteristically jocular mood.

But the old woman said nothing, and presently she began to help Kamakichi sift through a pile of ash. She worked with the deftness of a farm girl trained to sort beans of different sizes. As her fingers sifted, her mouth in ceaseless motion began to form words that she muttered to herself. "You poor, poor things. Whose bones are you, here in this miserable place? Look what's become of you. Who were your parents? And who were your children? It's all so sad."

Her mutterings were like a pesky gadfly that flitted about Kamakichi's ears. As he watched the deft movements of the old woman's withered hands, suddenly he was reminded of his mother. And then he remembered the three stones she had told him about. She said she had collected them at the bottom of the precipice at Mabuni. That was the place where Japanese soldiers had jumped to their deaths rather than surrender to the enemy at the end of the Battle of Okinawa. But he knew that the story about the stones was no more true than the inscription "June 23rd," the last day of the battle, that was written on the back of his father's mortuary tablet as the date of his death in the war. He recalled the photograph placed on the family altar of his father dressed in the uniform for civilians in the Okinawa Defense Corps. His father had been taken from his job at the town office and conscripted into this citizens' army, which was supposed to be the island's last line of defense. It had all happened so very long ago that, to Kamakichi, it seemed like some ancient, mythical tale that had no connection with him now.

Just as the men were about to finish for the day, the construction boss showed up. The straps of his safety helmet were, as always, tied firmly in place, and there was a folding ruler in his breast pocket.

"Looks like it's going to take a lot longer than expected." There was an arch look on his face as he peered down at the men in the pit.

"Look at it, will you? There are thousands of bones down here." Such was the cheerless reply the assistant section chief shouted back from the bottom of the hole.

Hippie-Beard shoveled a spadeful of bone and ash over the edge of the pit. "Wiping the ass of people who make a mess starting a war is no picnic, you know."

"This area here will be the front of the hotel's stroll garden," announced the construction boss as he walked around the pit one more time. "The landscape design is going to be quite elaborate."

"The view will be wonderful," said the assistant section chief, picking up on what the boss said and complimenting him.

"That's why, starting tomorrow, if it's okay with you, we'll get to work with the heavy equipment in the area next to your crew. As things stand now, we're way behind schedule, and it's time to start construction on the hotel."

"That's fine with us," replied the assistant section chief without a moment's hesitation.

That night Kamakichi sat drinking *awamori* at an *o–den* restaurant in Sakae-machi. It was his first night out in quite a while. But he had no appetite. It was almost as though his stomach were no longer his own. The mutterings of the old turtle woman continued to resound in his ears no matter how hard he tried to tune them out. Little by little, and long before he realized it, he had drunk himself into an alcoholic haze. He thought of his father, and the memories came back fast and furious, without letting up.

The bulldozer went to work in the area adjacent to the pit on the crew's third day at the site. The loud, ferocious roar and the perpetual cloud of dust it generated assaulted the men mercilessly. Their mouths filled with grit, and they began to feel sick. It was as though something had swept them up in the air and was shaking their internal organs violently. To make matters worse, what had been the sole source of pleasure in their lugubrious task was now denied them because the bulldozer obliterated all possibility of conversation. Indeed, it stamped out anything they tried to say in much the same way it trampled the weeds growing on the hillside. The men now fell into a dark, sullen mood, and as the temperature climbed and their fatigue increased, they became wildly careless wielding their shovels. As they spat and tried to clear their parched throats, they felt a rising anger directed in equal parts at the steel-monster bulldozer and the idiocy of the assistant section chief.

The old woman was back again to help, having arrived

in the morning. On the one hand, the din generated by what she called "the bull" made it impossible to hear her and thereby saved Kamakichi from having to listen to her gadfly-like mutterings. On the other hand, the lack of conversation or any other diversion left him all the more vulnerable to his private fantasies about the bones, causing him to withdraw into ever-deeper introspection.

It was a little past noon when the men began to uncover bones in the shape of whole skeletons. If not apparent earlier, it was now all too clear that excavating the grave site would be far more time consuming than originally anticipated. The bones were solid, each one a heavy weight. In addition, buried along with them were all sorts of paraphernalia. Metal helmets. Army boots. Canteens. Bayonets. The mouth of the pit looked like a battlefield strewn with the litter of war.

All the bones had turned a rusty red. Collarbones. Shoulder bones. Thighbones. Rib bones. Tailbones. Skulls. One after another, bones like those Kamakichi remembered seeing in high-school science class were chucked over the edge of the pit. Each time he went to pick one up, he could not prevent his mind from clothing it in fantasies about the living human flesh to which it had once been attached; and when he went to toss it in the burlap bag, he could not avoid hearing the dry, hollow sound it made. At times it seemed to him as if the bones were quietly laughing, their laughter not unlike the sound of a stone rolling over and over, or of a cricket chirping.

A skull cracked in two right before his eyes. As he looked at the jagged edges, he felt he was about to be sick. He had been suffering from a hangover since morning and was sure his stomach was about to go on a rampage. In the midday heat, his head felt terribly heavy.

A tattered pair of army boots was slung over the edge of the pit. As Kamakichi went to set them aside, he saw a perfect set of foot bones inside. Each and every white piece of bone was intact, arranged in five neat little rows. As he began to pull them out, he heard one bone that had stuck to the boot's inside sole snap and break off with a crisp, popping sound. He felt his fingers go numb. And suddenly, his chest began to heave. The nausea swept over him like a great wave that rose from his stomach and then surged forward.

The old woman was collecting skulls from which she painstakingly wiped the dirt. No matter what skull she picked up, it always seemed to have the look of a living human face. Although everything else had turned a rusty red, the teeth eerily retained their original shining white. It was if they were alive and wanted Kamakichi to know how hungry they were. He remembered the words his mother had said so many times. "War is hell. And, in that hell, no one escapes becoming a hungry ghost." She, too, had known what it was to fall into that hell and live among the hungry ghosts. Once, at the bottom of a dark cave at Makabe, she had taken a fistful of dirt and stuffed it into her little boy's mouth. Kamakichi was just a baby. He would not stop crying, and this was the only way she could silence him. She had seen a Japanese army officer silhouetted in the light at the mouth of the cave. His sword was drawn, and she knew that meant he would kill the child if he did not stop crying. And so it had become her habit to say to her son, "That's what war is like."

Doubtless these people had been on the verge of starvation when they died, and even now the bones wore a hungry look. Kamakichi's hands ceased to move, and kneeling there in front of a skull he mentally traced on it what he could remember of his father's face.

Just then a canteen came rolling over the edge of the pit. Casually, Kamakichi picked it up, then realized he could hear water still splashing inside. He felt as if his face had been dashed with cold water, and a terrible chill ran down his spine.

At the 3:00 P.M. break the assistant section chief asked if the men had come across any gold fillings. The engine on the heavy-duty equipment owned by Toa Electric had been switched off, but still the men made no effort to reply. "It's amazing. All these bones and not one gold-capped tooth in the lot. I wonder why." The answer to this question he had posed like some mysterious riddle was patently obvious, but something kept the men from speaking up. It required too much energy.

That was when Kamakichi happened to notice a flat piece of bone sitting right in front of him. It was shaped like a spatula, and a fragment of rusted metal protruded from its surface. When he picked it up and looked at it closely, he could see that a sharply pointed blade had pierced all the way through to the other side. "It must have hurt like hell," he said, muttering almost to himself. Even he was shaken by the implication of his own words.

What was that? Suddenly he was overcome by a hallucination that his father was lying right next to him. Yes, there he was, lying on his side. Kamakichi had never thought much about his father until now. It had always seemed natural for his father not to be around. Except once—and that was when he had gone for an interview at the bank and they had rejected him for the job. He had resented being a son with a father who had never been more than a fleeting figure—a ghost—in his life.

Before anyone knew it, the construction boss was back, standing around and talking with the assistant section chief. It appeared they were discussing the next step in the project. Since there was no sign that "the bull" was about to start up again, the men in the city hall work crew stretched out and decided to relax for a while.

"Cut it down?" They could hear the high-pitched voice of the assistant section chief.

"The landscape people will be here tomorrow to do their survey, and we can't wait any longer. We're way behind schedule."

"But what a waste. You can't just cut down a tree as big as this one. And didn't you say this spot was going to be part of the hotel garden?"

"But that's exactly why it's in the way. Besides, it's only a local tree that grew here naturally. We'll be bringing in coconut and fern palms as part of the garden's motif."

The assistant section chief made no attempt to question the construction boss further.

"Since it has to be cut down, we might as well do it now," the construction boss said. "Then, starting tomorrow, we'll put up a tent over there for shade at break times."

"Damn it. This is an outrage! It's out-and-out violence, that's what it is. Now you've gone too far." Suddenly Hippie-Beard had leapt to his feet.

Startled by the young man's voice, everyone started to

get up. But his expected protest did not last. And, looking as cool as could be, the construction boss ignored him.

"Our company has no intention of doing anything to inconvenience you."

Just then, the old turtle woman pushed her way through the men and stepped to the front of the group.

"Well, Mr. Bossman. You say you're going to chop down the banyan tree? And just who do you think it belongs to? That tree there was planted by my father. What's more, it has come to be possessed by the spirits of thousands of dead people. That's where their spirits live. Don't you have any common sense?"

There was something of the shaman about the old woman. Her raised eyebrows floating high on her forehead and her old, yellowed eyes coated with moisture gave her the look of a woman possessed.

"I can't say I know much about the customs in these parts," said the construction boss. "Besides, the title to the land has already been transferred, and . . ."

"I'll never permit it. Never. Because this tree here is my father's. Don't you have any appreciation for all the hardship and suffering people had to go through in the past?"

"We can't allow you to interfere with our job. No matter what you say."

The men continued to stand where they were, silent and expressionless. The construction boss's face was full of anger as his eyes surveyed, one by one, the apathetic faces in a row before him.

At last the assistant section chief spoke. "Isn't it possible to move the tree somewhere else?"

"There'd be no problem, if it were all that easy. But look, I only work for somebody else, just like you."

The turtle woman stepped between the two men. "Look here, you. If you so much as lay a finger on that tree, there will be a curse on you wherever you go in Okinawa, and, before you know it, bad luck will come crashing down on that head of yours."

Kamakichi leaned back against the banyan tree as he studied the withered nape of the old woman's neck. Given his druthers, it was a scene he would have preferred never to witness. How much better it would have been if he had averted his eyes and looked the other way. He felt his head grow feverish, and from time to time a knot tightened in his chest that made him feel as if he were going to be sick at any moment.

The surface of the banyan tree was rough to the touch, and it hurt when he rubbed his back against the trunk. Still, there was something about the tree that made him feel cool and refreshed. It made him think of his father again.

For no apparent reason he reached up and tore a single leaf from the branch overhead. Almost automatically his fingers went to work, and after trimming off the edges, he rolled the leaf up. Then, pinching one end of the rolled leaf between his fingers, he blew through it as hard as he could. The piercing screech it made took everyone by surprise. Even the construction boss's yellow safety helmet appeared to flash and—*bang!*—explode in the bright sunlight as he turned toward the sound of the whistle.

Translated by William J. Tyler

JEFFREY ANGLES is an assistant professor and head of the Japanese language program at Western Michigan University. His translations have appeared in *The Columbia Anthology of Modern Japanese Literature*, *Critical Asian Studies*, and numerous other journals. His current research focuses on representations of sexuality in Japanese literature of modernist era.

J. THOMAS RIMER, professor emeritus of Japanese literature at the University of Pittsburgh, has translated and written commentaries on Japanese literature from both the classical and modern periods. His latest publication is *The Columbia Anthology of Modern Japanese Literature*, co-edited with Van Gessel.

LAWRENCE ROGERS is professor of Japanese and chair of the department of Languages at the University of Hawai'i at Hilo, where he teaches Japanese language and literature. He has translated the novel *Citadel in Spring* by Agawa Hiroyuki and numerous short stories by contemporary authors. His collection *Tokyo Stories: A Literary Stroll* was awarded the 2004 translation prize by Columbia University's Donald Keene Center of Japanese Culture.

DENNIS KEENE was born in London and lived for many years in Tokyo, where he taught English literature. He has published two volumes of his own poetry, *Surviving* and *Universe,* and the literary study *Yokomitsu Riichi, Modernist.* His numerous translations of contemporary Japanese literature include the novels of Kita Morio, Maruya Saiichi, Nakamura Minoru, and Ikezawa Natsuki, as well as the poetry of Miyoshi Tatsuji, Anzai Fuyue, Tamura Ryūichi, Yoshioka Minoru, Tanikawa Shuntarō, and Inoue Yasushi. He currently lives in Oxford.

STEPHEN W. KOHL is an associate professor of Japanese at the University of Oregon. Translations include *The Saint of Mt. Koya* and the *Song of the Troubadour* by Izumi Kyōka, often referred to as a modern gothic writer, and *Wind and Stone* by the Korean-born Tachihara Masaaki. Recently, he has designed a website, complete with commentary, on Matsuo Bashō's haiku travelogue *Oku no hosomichi* (The Narrow Road to the Far North), and he has been researching narratives and diaries written by Japanese castaways.

BURTON WATSON is a prolific translator of numerous works of poetry, prose, historiography, and philosophy from both Chinese and Japanese. He has translated numerous classical Chinese poets, including Po Chü-I, Du Fu, Su Tung-Po, and Han Shan, and produced English renditions of many critically important Buddhist sutras, including *The Lotus Sutra*. Among his translations from Japanese are books of the short stories of Oda Sakunosuke and the poetry of Masaoka Shiki. His latest translation, *The Tale of the Heike*, the classic Japanese medieval tale, will be published in the summer of 2006 by Columbia University Press.

ANTHONY HOOD CHAMBERS is a professor of Japanese literature at Arizona State University. He has translated a number of modern and pre-modern texts, most notably several novels by Tanizaki Jun'ichirō, including *The Secret History of the Lord of Musashi*, *Arrowroot*, *The Reed Cutter*, *Captain Shigemoto's Mother*, and *Naomi*, and has produced as well a study entitled *The Secret Window: Ideal Worlds in Tanizaki's Fiction*. His translation of the eighteenth-century classic *Tales of Moonlight and Rain*, by Ueda Akinari, is forthcoming from Columbia University Press.

MILLICENT M. HORTON earned an M.A. in Japanese literature at the University of California at Los Angeles in 1971 and later studied at the University of Hawaii. She is the translator of *The Square Persimmon and Other Stories* by Atōda Takashi.

MARK HARBISON is the translator of several books about Japanese art and culture, including *Ukiyo-e: An Introduction to Japanese Woodblock Prints* and *Utamaro: Portraits from the Floating World*, both by art historian Kobayashi Takashi, and *The Anatomy of Self: The Individual Versus Society* by psychologist Doi Takeo. After living in Japan for many years and teaching at the University of Tokyo, he now lives in Hawaii, where he sells real estate with his wife.

KYOKO OMORI is an assistant professor in the East Asian Languages and Literatures Department of Hamilton College. She has published a translation of a short story by Tani Jōji, the mystery novelist and creator of the "'Merican-Jap" series from the 1920s, in *The Columbia Anthology of Modern Japanese Literature*. Her introductory essay and translations of selected entries from the journals of Higuchi Ichiyō are forthcoming in *The Modern Murasaki: Selected Works by Women Writers of Meiji Japan, 1885–1912*. She is working on a book project titled *Detecting Modanizumu: New Youth Magazine, Mystery Fiction, and the Culture of Japanese Vernacular Modernism, 1920–1950*.

MICHAEL EMMERICH is the translator of numerous books from Japanese, including *First Snow on Fuji* by the Nobel-Prize winner Kawabata Yasunari, *Sayonara, Gangsters* by the postmodern writer Takahashi Gen'ichirō, and *Asleep*, *Goodbye Tsugumi*, and *Hardboiled and Hardluck*, all by the popular young writer Yoshimoto Banana. He is currently a PhD candidate in pre-modern Japanese literature at Columbia University.

WILLIAM J. TYLER is an associate professor of Japanese Language and Literature at Ohio State University. He has published two volumes by the modernist writer Ishikawa Jun: *The Bodhisattva, or Samantabhadra* and *The Legend of Gold and Other Stories*, both containing translations and extended critical analyses. He is the editor of the volume *Modanizumu in Japanese Fiction: An Introduction to Modernist Prose from Japan, 1914–1938*, a forthcoming collection of twenty-five works by seventeen authors.